Transforming Government and Public Services

To all those who are 'doing the right thing'.

Transforming Government and Public Services

Realising Benefits through Project Portfolio Management

STEPHEN JENNER

LONDON AND NEW YORK

First published in paperback 2024

First published 2010 by Gower Publishing

Published 2016 by Routledge
4 Park Square, Milton Park, Abingdon, Oxon OX14 4RN

and by Routledge
605 Third Avenue, New York, NY 10158

Routledge is an imprint of the Taylor & Francis Group, an informa business

British Library Cataloguing in Publication Data
Jenner, Stephen.
  Transforming government and public services : realising
  benefits through project portfolio management.
  1. Public administration. 2. Portfolio management.
  I. Title
  352.4'39-dc22

Library of Congress Cataloging-in-Publication Data
Jenner, Stephen.
  Transforming government and public services : realising benefits through project portfolio management / by Stephen Jenner.
     p. cm.
  Includes bibliographical references and index.
  ISBN 978-1-4094-0163-6 (hbk.) -- ISBN 978-1-4094-0307-4 (ebook)
  1. Public administration--Management. 2. Project management. I. Title.
  JF1351.J46 2010
  352.3'65--dc22

                                                                      2009050640

ISBN 13: 978-1-4094-0163-6 (hbk)
ISBN 13: 978-1-03-283846-5 (pbk)
ISBN 13: 978-1-315-55009-1 (ebk)

DOI: 10.4324/9781315550091

Contents

List of Figures

Acknowledgements

I am indebted to the following professional colleagues for their advice and for contributing examples used in this book: Dr Achilleas Mavrellis (Defra), Kevin Fletcher (Manchester City Council), Warren Fraser (Queensland University of Technology), Paul Jackson (Advisor, CIPFA Networks), Kenna Kintrea and Ky Nichol (Olympic Delivery Authority), Bengt Nilsson (Tetra Pak), San Retna (chair of the Enterprise Portfolio Management Council), Anand Sanwal (Corporate Portfolio Management Association) and Terry Wright (Department of Treasury and Finance, Victoria, Australia).

Leading academics who have helped in the formulation of the concepts that appear throughout this book include: Bent Flyvbjerg (BT Professor and Chair of Major Programme Management, Saïd Business School, Oxford), Bob Cooper (McMaster University, Canada), Catherine Killen (University of Technology, Sydney, Australia), John Ward (Cranfield University) and Dr Peter Beven (Queensland University of Technology).

Professional colleagues in Government who have influenced my thinking include: Bob Assirati and Michael Acaster at the OGC, Martin Crumpton (DfT), Dr Helen Goulding (Audit Commission), Paul Hirst (HMRC), Nick Walker (DCSF), Bryan Lee (NOMS), David Palmer (Home Office), Sue Harding (Department for Work and Pensions) and numerous colleagues on the cross Government Tell Us Once programme including Lyn McDonald, Matt Briggs and Julie Brown; and in the Ministry of Justice, Louise Woodford, Joan Lewis, Carole Sullivan and Dan Colborne. Above all, John Suffolk, UK Government CIO, made much of this possible with his support and encouragement. In Australia, I should also pay credit to, among many others, Michelle Hendy, Sabrina Walsh, Mark Browning and Ross Garland.

The contribution of colleagues from the private sector is also recognised, and in particular the following from the Enterprise Portfolio Management Council: San Retna, Michael Stratton, Mark Wybraniec, Diane Miller, Michael Menke, Michael Mee, Mark Stabler, Michael Gosnear and Sarma Tekumalla. I should also specifically mention John Thorp (not least for his thought-provoking blogs, continued enthusiasm and optimism) Shan Rajegopal and Craig Kilford for keeping it fun and cool.

The early research for this book was informed by contributions from colleagues in the United States Federal Government and in Australia, most notably, Tracey Edwards (Queensland) and Terry Wright in Victoria. The conclusions of that research were also discussed with Gartner analysts and researchers Matt Light, Audrey Apfel, John Kost and David McClure, and I am happy to acknowledge the value of their time and insight. I should also mention Simon Greener, Rachi Weerasinghe and Jason Whitfield for their efforts in organising the Public Sector Programme and Portfolio Management Club.

Special thanks go to members of the CJS IT Portfolio Unit who contributed their hearts and minds to the development of the ideas, concepts and tools described in this book, and in particular – Jonathan Fearon, Jennifer Wallace, Monica Hiew, Stuart Bromwich, Jill Thibaut, Rob Davis, Peter Wright, Christopher Munday, Gareth Bell, Tim Laken and Michaela Chilcott. Proof if ever there was that quality surpasses quantity every time. Then there are those that provided independent advice and support – most notably Jon Chadwick (CapGemini) my own 'devil's advocate', Rob Parker (Pcubed) the model independent facilitator discussed in Chapter 4, and Karen Farquharson and Simon Wilson (Proving Services).

I thank my mother, Pamela, and sister, Sue for their continuing apparent interest in my ramblings. Most of all though, my daughters Carly and Kareena, son Max and last, but never least, my wife Patricia who constantly reminds me what value really is.

Glossary

Achievability	Or risk in relation to technical achievability, project deliverability and the likelihood of benefits realisation.
Analytical Hierarchy Process	A method used in portfolio selection and options appraisal based on pair-wise comparisons. Its use is aided by appropriate computer software. Often used in conjunction with Decision Conferencing – see below.
Affordability	Whether funding, both capital and resource/operating, exists to fund the full life costs of the project.
Attractiveness	The potential return from an investment in terms of: financial or performance impact, or in terms of maintaining business as usual, or meeting a legal or regulatory requirement.
Benefits Management	The process that seeks to ensure that: • the benefits used to justify an investment are robust and realisable; • all potential forms of value are recognised; and • benefits realisation is actively managed to ensure the performance matches the promise, emergent benefits are captured and disseminated, and capability and capacity created is leveraged to create additional value.
Business case	A document which explores the rationale for investment and the options for achieving the desired business outcomes. Usually prepared in the five case format promoted by the OGC – Strategic Case, Economic Case, Financial Case, Commercial Case and Project Management Case.
Champion Challenger process	A process where stakeholders are actively encouraged to propose enhancements to the existing process ('challengers') which if accepted, become the new 'champion' process to be used by all.
Change Portfolio Diagnostic Assessment Model.	An approach to assessing capability encompassing key portfolio management processes augmented by consideration of the dimensions of governance and behaviour. It is based on key principles rather than preset fixed definitions of what constitutes, for example, level 3 as opposed to level 4 in 'Investment Management'. In this way, the model is used not to assess an organisation against a definition of what maturity means at each level, but rather to engage key stakeholders in a dialogue to determine what good looks like for an organisation given its specific circumstances at a point in time.
Decision Conferencing	A process by which portfolio prioritisation and selection decisions are made collectively 'in conference'. Often used in conjunction with multi-criteria analysis. The advantages of this approach include not only a shared commitment to portfolio selection decisions, but also to the portfolio management process since participants help select and weight the investment criteria used. Success is highly dependent on skilled facilitation.

Discounted cash flows	Cost and Revenue in future periods adjusted to today's value using the organisation's cost of capital (3.5 per cent in central government).
EGAP-principle	The practice of appraising projects on the basis of forecasts prepared on the assumption that 'everything goes according to plan' – which of course is rarely the case. (Source: World Bank).
Green book	The HM Treasury publication *Appraisal and Evaluation in Central Government* which constitutes binding guidance for government departments and executive agencies.
Internal Rate of Return	*'The annual percentage return achieved by a project, at which the sum of the discounted cash inflows over the life of the project is equal to the sum of the discounted cash outflows.'* (Source: CIMA, Management Accounting Official Terminology, 2000 edition).
Investment appraisal	*Ex ante* analysis of a project or programme to determine whether investment is justified and to select the most appropriate option for meeting the identified business need.
Investment evaluation	*Ex post* analysis to determine whether the project or programme was delivered as planned and whether the forecast benefits have been received (summative evaluation) and how additional value can be created and what lessons can be leant to improve delivery and benefits realisation in the future (formative evaluation).
Mandatory projects	Projects mandated by law, regulation or the need to maintain business as usual.
Maturity Model	A model for assessing an organisation's capability against identified good practice across a range of process areas, for example, P3M3. See also Change Portfolio Diagnostic Assessment Model.
Modular projects	Defined by the Cabinet Office (2000) 'Successful IT: Modernising Government in Action' as '*a discrete part of an overall programme of work that offers some value to the organisation, even if the other parts of the programme are not completed'.*
Multi-Criteria Analysis	The use of financial and other relevant criteria in investment appraisal and portfolio prioritisation decisions. Typically, identified criteria are weighted and projects are ranked according to their weighted scores against these criteria. Often used in conjunction with Decision Conferencing.
Net Present Value (NPV).	The value of future net cash flows (outflows less inflows) discounted at the relevant cost of capital (3.5 per cent in UK central government). Where the cash outflows exceed the inflows the result is the 'Net Present Cost' or NPC.
Optimism bias	The HM Treasury Green Book states that, '*There is a demonstrated, systemic tendency for project appraisers to be overly optimistic. This is a worldwide phenomenon that affects both the private and public sectors... appraisers tend to overstate benefits, and understate timings and costs, both capital and operational.'*
Payback	The period of time before the cash inflows from an investment exceed the accumulated cash outflows. Can be calculated using discounted or undiscounted cash flows.

Planning fallacy	The belief that your project will progress as forecast whilst also being aware that many similar projects suffer from time slippage, cost escalation and benefits shortfalls.
Portfolio Balance	When the portfolio is balanced in terms of: projects and programmes at various stages of their life cycles; coverage of strategic priorities; a mix of longer-term capacity enhancing investments and those with a more immediate return; in terms of scale; risk; capability to deliver; and business change impact.
Portfolio Dashboards	A mechanism to monitor and report portfolio performance encompassing measures of: Delivery, Efficiency, Balance and Impact.
Portfolio Management Office	Function responsible for developing, implementing and operating the Portfolio Management process.
Portfolio Management Process	Encompasses four sub-processes: • Establishing the portfolio • Investment Appraisal and Portfolio Selection • Managing the Portfolio in flight • Benefits Realisation.
Portfolio Map	A chart used to show the relative attractiveness and achievability of potential and actual investments.
Portfolio Reviews	Periodic review of the portfolio in aggregate – to ensure that it remains strategically aligned, balanced, and continues to represent the optimum 'bang' for our investment 'buck'.
Portfolio Segmentation	Splitting the portfolio into organisationally appropriate categories, for example, by project type and/or investment objective – and then tailoring the investment criteria to the various portfolio segments.
Productivity Index	Net Present Value per unit of limiting factor.
Programme	A collection of projects and other activities that are managed in a coordinated manner in order to achieve some overall desired outcome and benefits realisation.
Project	Defined by the OGC's *Managing Successful Programmes* as, '*A particular way of managing activities to deliver specific outputs over a specified period and within cost, quality and resource constraints.*'
Project and Programme Management (PPM)	The discipline of 'doing projects/programmes right', that is, ensuring delivery on time, to budget, to agreed specifications, and in terms of benefits realisation.
Project Portfolio	The collection of projects and programmes planned and 'in flight' at any one time.
Project Portfolio Management (PPfM)	The discipline of managing the selection and delivery of an organisation's collection of projects and programmes to optimise the return on investment and portfolio balance within resource constraints, and in the context of organisational and environmental change.

Project Portfolio Prioritisation	The process of prioritising and selecting the optimum mix or collection of projects and programmes in terms of their: • *Return or Attractiveness* – maximising impact, including financial returns and contribution to strategic objectives and business priorities; • *Risk or Achievability* – ensuring that the collection of change initiatives is deliverable, that constraints (including availability of skilled resources) and dependencies, are effectively managed, and that the overall business change requirement is manageable; and • *Affordability* – both upfront investment and ongoing running costs.
Reference class forecasting	Where project estimates of cost, time and benefit are derived from what actually occurred in a reference class of similar projects rather than being built up from an understanding of the specific project alone.
Stage or phase gate reviews	Reviews undertaken at specified points in the project life cycle encompassing: *A backward look*: progress since the last gate review – has 'progress matched the promise', have the required actions been addressed and has spending stayed within the approved budgetary envelope? *A forward look*: the revised forecast cost/benefit position – how attractive is the project in financial and business value terms and how reliable are the forecasts?, an updated assessment of achievability and identification of key issues and obstacles and what actions are required by the project and the business to improve the likelihood of success?
Start gate	An initial concept screening process or 'start gate'. This ensures that all initiatives entering the change portfolio meet minimum standards of attractiveness and achievability as well as considering their impact on, and fit with, the portfolio (existing and planned) as a whole.
Strategic Contribution Analysis	A technique for determining a project's strategic contribution by combining: • a Strategy Map – a description of the organisation's Vision, the strategies used to attain that Vision and the measures used to assess achievement of the strategies; with • a Benefits Map/Model showing the benefits to be realised from change initiatives – and how these benefits contribute to the strategic measures identified above.
Strategic Misrepresentation	A term coined by Bent Flyvbjerg to refer to the planned, systematic distortion or misstatement of the costs and benefits used to justify an investment. It is seen as a rational response to incentives in the investment appraisal process. Addressing it calls for a combination of: independent scrutiny and validation of proposals; reference class forecasting; aligning incentives with more accurate forecasting; and improved accountability from tracking performance.
'Sunk' cost	Costs already incurred and which are therefore not relevant to an investment decision.
Triangulation	Using more than one appraisal method, or 'value lens', to assess the business case. Thus economic appraisal may be combined with financial appraisal, Multi Criteria Analysis and Strategic Contribution Analysis.
Value Management Office (VMO)	A unit established with the remit to ensure that the organisation optimises the return from its change portfolio.

Foreword

Any organisation that invests in business change does so to realise benefits based on the investment they make – in terms of efficiency improvements, contributions to strategic targets and business priorities, maintaining business critical operations or to meet mandatory legal and regulatory requirements.

The vehicle by which such change is most often achieved is project and programme management. Yet reports and research consistently show that organisations, both here and abroad, and in the private as well as the public sectors, struggle to demonstrate that they have realised the potential benefits from these investments in change. The reality is that whilst improvements in project and programme management disciplines have improved our ability to consistently deliver individual initiatives on time and to budget, we also need to look more widely at our approaches to:

- prioritising available investment funds to areas of greatest impact and updating this in the light of environmental and organisational change;

- successfully managing the delivery of the organisation's entire collection of change initiatives; and

- maximising the benefits realised from our accumulated investment in change.

My experience over 30 years in both public and private sectors, including leading major IT-enabled transformation programmes, is that success depends on five key fundamentals:

- Firstly, there needs to be clarity about what success will look like and everyone needs to have a shared understanding of this and what their role in it is – in short, we need a clear line of sight from strategic intent to benefits realisation and to individuals' performance objectives.

- Secondly, as boring as this may sound, repeatable processes lay the basis for success. They are insufficient on their own, but I have yet to see a successful organisation that does not also have clear, repeatable processes that are adhered to – after all, it doesn't sound right that successful organisations make it up as they go along.

- Thirdly, we need to be hungry for information that helps us understand how successfully we are delivering change, what impact that investment in change is having in terms of benefits realisation, and if there are emerging issues, what are the underlying causes and consequently what management action is required? A 'single version of the truth' helps enormously here.

- Fourthly, with clarity about success and a clear line of sight, comes commitment to the cause. Hearts, as well as minds, need to be engaged, and this depends on continuous participative engagement so that people understand the rationale for the change and what quantifiable difference it will make. Remembering that memories are short, get used to saying the same thing over and over again.

- Finally, and above all, we need to deliver value for money – the return, however we measure it, needs to exceed the cost of the investment.

This is the domain of value-led Project Portfolio Management which combines three distinct disciplines – investment management (ensuring we invest and significantly, continue to invest, to optimise the 'bang' from our limited 'buck'); project and programme management (ensuring we deliver on time and to budget across the change portfolio); and benefits realisation management (ensuring we realise all potential value from our investments – not think we do on paper but actually do in our pockets).

As this book shows, this is a relatively new discipline both here in the UK and abroad. The good news is that organisations have developed tools, techniques and approaches that others can use to fast track themselves to improved performance. This book distills the learnings from practical experience and academic research and as such it represents a significant contribution to the challenges we face in transforming government and public services in an environment of ever-tighter finances.

John Suffolk, UK Government CIO

Preface

The pressure on the public sector to deliver improved services, become more customer focused, and at the same time, to realise efficiency savings has never been greater – and all at a time of shrinking budgets and rising citizen and business expectations. The UK Government's 2005 'Transformational Government – Enabled by Technology'[1] strategy put the use of technology at the heart of public service reform and committed the UK Government to:

- the transformation of public services for the benefit of citizens, businesses, taxpayers and front line staff;

- more efficient services thus freeing resources for the front line; and

- more effective delivery and management of the Government's investment in IT, including adopting a portfolio management approach.

This was followed by Sir David Varney's review of Service Transformation in 2006, which culminated in the 'Service Transformation Agreement' in late 2007[2] with the aim of changing *public services so they more often meet the needs of people and businesses, rather than the needs of government, and by doing so reduce the frustration and stress of accessing them. The result will be services that are better for the customer, better for front line staff and better for the taxpayer*. More recently in the UK we have had the Operational Efficiency and Public Value Programmes with their challenging targets for delivering more with less.

Transformational change programmes are consequently increasingly common across government, with similar agendas in other leading economies as evidenced by the case studies and examples cited throughout this book. The risks of failure have however never been greater as the scale of change

---

1   Cabinet Office (2005) *Transformational Government Enabled by Technology*, Available at: http://www.cabinetoffice.gov.uk/media/141734/transgov-strategy.pdf [Last accessed: 30th December 2009].

2   HM Government (2007) *Service Transformation Agreement*, Available at: http://www.hm-treasury.gov.uk/d/pbr_csr07_service.pdf [Last accessed: 13th December 2008].

required to move organisations from the 'as is' to the 'to be' position expands. Scale of change is not the only problem, complexity is a real issue – in many cases strategy, and consequently the programmes designed to deliver them, are emergent, that is, there is no fixed point to which we can work. Additionally such programmes encompass technology, business processes and aspects of 'people change' (including the skills and location of those providing the services) and these elements need to be managed simultaneously rather than sequentially. These changes also often cross organisational boundaries and there is the ever-present need to respond to shifts in policy and new legislation.

The result is that, in practice, many organisations in both the public and private sectors have struggled to manage optimally their collection, or portfolio, of investments in change. The consequences are seen in reports of:

- too many projects soaking up management time, exceeding the organisation's capacity to deliver and to absorb change;

- initiatives that are no longer a strategic priority, or which are of uncertain value, but which nevertheless continue because no one really asks the questions, *'if we started now would we invest in this initiative?'* and *'is there a better way to invest our money?'*;

- portfolios that are unbalanced in terms of risk, scheduling and coverage of priorities;

- inefficient resource management leading to bottlenecks and/or slack – and either way, to inefficient use of scarce resources and, often, excessive reliance on expensive consultants and contractors; and

- performance not matching the promise in terms of project delivery and benefits realisation. Even when projects and programmes are delivered on time and to budget, organisations often struggle to demonstrate the realisation of the forecast benefits which were the rationale for the investment in the first place.

The challenges we face have been highlighted in recent reviews. A report by the National Audit Office in 2006[3] concluded that there must be a broadening

---

3 National Audit Office (17th November 2006) *Delivering Successful IT-enabled Business Change,* Available at: http://www.nao.org.uk/publications/0607/delivering_successful_it-enabl.aspx [Last accessed: 13th December 2008].

and deepening of Government's professionalism in terms of the planning, delivery and governance of IT-enabled change. This included departments managing their portfolios of projects and programmes, establishing a clear overview of the range of business change activities planned or underway, and assessing capacity to manage the change. This theme was further emphasised in the UK Government's progress report on the Capability Reviews[4] in late 2007. The report identified one of the biggest delivery challenges for departments as being, '*Prioritisation. When asked what would make the most difference to enabling change to happen, the most common factor identified by the SCS* [Senior Civil Service] *was "clear objectives" – "real prioritization...Factors hindering change included 'too many competing priorities" and a, "lack of common objectives and prioritization."'* A report from the HM Treasury Financial Skills Advisory Panel in early 2008 concluded that the key challenges facing government include, '*The reluctance/failure to prioritise, to stop some activities in order to create headroom and release resources for new initiatives.*'[5] Most recently, the Operational Efficiency Programme from HM Treasury (April 2009) has included the commitment to implement '*portfolio management processes within departments to prioritise the most important IT-enabled change projects and resources and to reduce the overlap and duplication in IT-enabled change projects across the public sector*'.[6] But as I say above, these challenges extend beyond the public sector and the UK.

Whilst project and programme management (also referred to as PPM) disciplines are relevant to delivery and the question, '*are we doing projects right?*', project portfolio management (also referred to as PPfM) asks whether we are doing, and more to the point, continue to do '*the right projects*' in terms of optimising financial savings, operational efficiencies and performance improvements. For the sake of brevity, I have decided to stick with the commonly used title 'project portfolio management' but to be clear, this is not restricted to formally constituted projects, but rather also includes programmes and other change initiatives.

The good news is that real progress has been made – public sector organisations are addressing the challenges outlined above by employing portfolio management techniques to the management of their change

---

4   HM Government (December 2007) *Capability Reviews: Progress and Next Steps.*
5   HM Government (February 2008) *Doing the Business Embedding Financial Management Skills in Government,* Available at: http://thegfp.treasury.gov.uk/resources/gfp/GFP%202008/2008 0208%20DTB%20-%20Embedding%20Financial%20Skills.pdf [Last accessed: 13th December 2008].
6   HM Treasury (2009) *Operational Efficiency Programme: Final Report,* Available at: http://www. hm-treasury.gov.uk/d/oep_final_report_210409_pu728.pdf [Last accessed 31st October 2009].

programmes. In this book I explore the case for project portfolio management, how the potential benefits can be realised, and the tools, techniques and processes that have been proven to work in complex transformational change programmes in both the UK and abroad. In so doing we explore the lessons learned from the practical application of these techniques in both the private and public sectors, as well as the evidence from academic and industry research. This experience includes that of the Criminal Justice System IT portfolio where the techniques adopted in this book won the 2007 Civil Service Financial Management award, as well as being recognised in case studies by industry research organisation Gartner,[7] and in reports to the OECD and European Commission.[8]

Book Overview

In Chapter 1 we explore the case for using portfolio management to manage our collection of change projects, programmes and initiatives, including a review of the evidence linking the application of portfolio management to improved performance.

Chapter 2 then explores the prerequisites that experience and research have shown to be crucial in implementing project portfolio management effectively. We also identify the two factors that are sometimes presumed to be prerequisites for project portfolio management but which it turns out are not necessary.

Chapters 3 to 6 then examine the four key process elements of project portfolio management in detail:

- Chapter 3. Establishing the Portfolio – its scope (what's 'in' and what's 'out') and procedures, guidelines and templates.

- Chapter 4. Deciding where to invest – prioritising and selecting investments at an individual and collective level to optimise our return on investment subject to considerations of achievability and

---

7   Di Maio, A. (2005) *UK Criminal Justice System Makes Portfolio Management Key to IT Success*, Gartner ID Number: G00130564.

8   Cabinet Office (13th February 2006) *UK Approach to Benefits Realisation, Country Report in Support of the eGovernment Expert Meeting on the Cost and Benefit Analysis of e-Government*, Final Version 0.11; and e Government Economics Project (e GEP) (1 March 2006) Compendium to the Measurement Framework. Also see the Case Study on the CIO website, Available at: http://www.cabinetoffice.gov.uk/cio/reliable_project_delivery/pm_cjit_case_study.aspx [Last accessed 30th December 2009].

affordability. We also consider the issue of the reliability (or not) of the data that underpins our investment decisions and the need for an improved balance between managerial judgment and data-driven decision making.

- Chapter 5. Managing the portfolio of projects and programmes 'in flight' on an active basis to ensure a balanced portfolio is maintained, with a high degree of strategic alignment, and to optimise the return on investment in the light of changing circumstances, both organisational and environmental.

- Chapter 6. Active Value Management, to ensure that all potential benefits are identified, that forecast benefits are realised, and to exploit capability and learning's to create additional value.

In Chapter 7 we review how project portfolio management can be most effectively implemented and how to sustain progress. This in turn requires that we look beyond process to the twin dimensions of governance and behaviour.

Chapter 8 examines how we might measure success both in process and performance terms. It also includes my suggested Change Portfolio Diagnostic Assessment Model.

We then finish with our conclusions in Chapter 9 including twenty top tips on implementing project portfolio management and sustaining progress.

To aid understanding, each chapter starts with a short summary of the areas to be covered and ends with a 'conclusions and takeaways' section. Throughout the book several key themes reappear – these represent the fundamental 'stakes in the ground' on which value-led project portfolio management is built:

- *'Starting with the end in mind'* – developing business cases to achieve the desired intent rather than to justify a particular solution. All costs required to realise the benefits forecast should be included in the business case.

- Establishing a *'clear line of sight'* from strategic intent through to benefits realisation. Too often the project documentation I see appears to be written 'by geniuses for geniuses'[9] – it may be

---

9   This term was originally used by John Suffolk on his appointment as Director General of CJIT.

technically strong, but users don't gain a clear understanding of the end state, why we want to get there or how we will get there.

- Treating projects as *investments* – being clear about *'what benefits you are buying'* and shifting the emphasis from a cost-based to a value-based business case where the focus is on *'what does it cost to buy these benefits?'*

- *'Validating and triangulating'* project appraisals and using more than one 'value lens' – to identify the 'assumptions that masquerade as facts'.[10]

- Using *'gates with teeth'* with incremental funding allocations linked to performance, realistic appraisals of the benefits to be realised and culminating in formal recommitment to the benefits case.

- *Planning for success* – portfolio management is an active discipline premised on joint accountability for performance rather than holding people to account after the event when the investment is 'sunk'.

- Utilising the *'one version of the truth'* principle in portfolio reporting to overcome arguments about the accuracy of the data.

- Employing summary documentation – short documents and reports (business cases, benefits reports and so on) convey the relevant facts far more effectively than long documents. Size, in this context, is the enemy of understanding. Wherever possible use single page reports.

The findings presented are derived from the author's experience in major change programmes and investment appraisal, and from research, including that undertaken to inform the development of project portfolio management as part of the 'Transformational Government' agenda. The solutions offered are consequently based on practical and research experience both here in the UK and abroad.

---

10 This term is borrowed from a presentation by Bob Mornan, then of the Canadian Government to the OECD in 2006.

1

The Case for Project Portfolio Management

'Show me the money.'

Jerry Maguire

After reading this chapter you will:

- understand what is meant by project portfolio management, its origins and development over the last 20 or so years;
- have an appreciation of the theoretical arguments that are made in support of a portfolio management approach and the potential benefits claimed;
- understand the evidence, both quantitative and qualitative, that supports the argument that portfolio management can improve project delivery, reduce risk and increase benefits realisation.

Introduction

In this chapter we examine the evidence for adopting a portfolio approach to managing an organisation's collection of change projects, programmes and initiatives, that is, what evidence is there that project portfolio management has a payback in terms of improved performance? But firstly, what do we mean by project portfolio management and what are the origins of the discipline?

The Office of Government Commerce (OGC)[1] defines portfolio management as *'a corporate, strategic level process for co-ordinating successful delivery across an organisation's entire set of programmes and projects...Portfolio Management at the corporate level provides an overview of the organisation's total investment such that:*

---

1   OGC (May 2004) *Portfolio Management* Version 1.0.

- *programmes and projects can be scrutinised and monitored to ensure ongoing alignment with strategic objectives and business imperatives;*

- *the broad allocation of skilled programme and project resources can be optimised;*

- *new requirements can be evaluated against current commitments;*

- *programme and project demands on operational business can be managed and co-ordinated at a corporate level.'*

The National Audit Office (NAO)[2] provides a similar, if more succinct definition: *'Prioritisation of all an organisation's programmes and projects in line with business objectives and matched to its capacity to deliver them.'*

What we see from both these definitions is that essentially portfolio management is about prioritising and selecting the optimum mix or collection of projects and programmes in terms of their:

- Return or Attractiveness – maximising impact, including financial returns and contribution to strategic objectives and business priorities; and

- Risk or Achievability – ensuring that the collection of change initiatives is deliverable, that constraints (including availability of skilled resources) and dependencies, are effectively managed, and that the overall business change impact is manageable.

All subject to the third 'A' of *Affordability* – matching the portfolio to the funding profile that is available over the planning period. As we shall see, this is not a once-off or annual planning exercise, rather it is an active, dynamic process in which resource allocation is continually adjusted to match project performance and changes in organisational priorities and the environment.

It should also be noted that portfolio management can be applied at different organisational levels, for example, at the corporate, departmental or business unit level. It can also be applied to different portfolios or collections of investments,

---

2   National Audit Office (17th November 2006) *Delivering successful IT-enabled business change*, Available at: http://www.nao.org.uk/publications/0607/delivering_successful_it-enabl.aspx [Last accessed: 13th December 2008].

for example, to Research and Development (R&D); Information Technology (existing IT assets and new projects); IT projects and programmes; and as is argued here, to the wider business change project and programme portfolio. Much of the research cited comes from the IT and R&D fields because these are the fields in which portfolio management has most often been applied to date. Indeed, a search on Google in July 2008 found 19.4m hits for IT project portfolio management and only 2.8m hits for project portfolio management, although, as we shall see, the disciplines and techniques employed are just as applicable to the transformational change portfolio as they are to the IT or R&D portfolios.

The Origins of Portfolio Management

Our story begins with a 1952 paper by Harry Markowitz.[3] Markowitz demonstrated that the application of portfolio theory to financial stocks and shares offered superior returns for a given level of risk or volatility in return. Indeed, subject to the usual caveats about past returns reflecting future returns (a problematic concept in the context of the recent credit crunch and market volatility), one is able to optimise return for any given level of risk so creating what is known as the 'efficient frontier' by diversifying away non-market risk. Markowitz won a Nobel Prize in 1990 for his work which has been widely adopted in the financial sector over the last half century.

Projects and programmes are however somewhat different in nature from financial securities, and, in particular, they lack the quantified data on traded values and volatility of returns on which the application of portfolio theory in financial markets is based. There is no active, liquid market in which a return on deselected investments can be realised and, on the contrary, there are significant switching costs for users associated with changing systems. Consideration of value needs to take account of non-financial and subjective factors which in turn mean decision making remains a balance of managerial judgment and data-driven analysis. Consequently, while the goals of project and financial portfolio management are similar (to optimise return for a given level of risk), the techniques used differ. Despite these differences there has been an increasing recognition in recent years that an approach that considers return in the context of risk (at both project and portfolio level), that seeks to manage organisational constraints such as resource availability and the capacity for organisational change across all change initiatives, and that focuses on benefits realisation throughout the project life cycle, has significant potential advantages.

---

3   Markowitz, H. (1952) 'Portfolio Selection', *Journal of Finance* 7:1, pp. 77–91.

The case for applying portfolio management to an organisation's project portfolio was first made in 1981 when Warren McFarlan[4] argued for a risk-based approach to selecting and managing IT projects both individually and as a portfolio. The next major milestone came in 1998 with John Thorp's *The Information Paradox*[5] and its focus on IT-enabled change. Since then, interest has continued to grow, encouraged, at least in part, by the claims of software vendors and consultants regarding the potential payback from implementing IT package solutions to manage project portfolios – for example:

- Primavera[6] claim benefits for government that include: *'Rationalization of existing investments that can result in near-term savings of 10–20 per cent of the portfolio's value'*.

- ChangeDirector[7] quote analyst research that: *'companies who adopt an integrated PPM solution can save 10 per cent of their total portfolio value per annum'* from *'increasing the certainty of benefits...Reducing wasted investments [and] improving the efficiency of the PMO'*.

- META Group report[8] that leveraging project portfolio management can realise a reduction of 20–30 per cent on project spending with no negative business impact and one telecomms provider achieved immediate cost savings of $600m.

- A Gartner analyst has been quoted as forecasting that organisations that implement and sustain a project portfolio management solution can save between 10 and 30 per cent of the total portfolio value p.a.[9]

- IBM Business Consulting Services claim overall project contingency could be reduced by up to 55 per cent.[10]

4   McFarlan, F. W. (1981) 'Portfolio Approach to Information Systems', *Harvard Business Review*, September–October 1981: pp. 142–151.
5   Thorp, J. (1998) *The Information Paradox*, McGraw-Hill, Canada.
6   http://www.primavera.com/products/prosight/government/prosight_gov.asp.
7   Breakfast Briefing, 6th December 2007.
8   Handler, R. (2 June 2003) 'Enterprise Program Management Office ROI SWAG', *META Practice*, Practice 2044.
9   Light, M. (2005) cited by ChangeDirector Breakfast Briefing 6th December 2007.
10 *Reaching Efficient Frontiers in IT Investment Management, What Financial Services CIOs can Learn from Portfolio Theory*, Available at: http://www-03.ibm.com/industries/financialservices/doc/content/bin/fss_bae_IT_management.pdf [Last accessed: 13th December 2008].

Whether such claims are supported by reliable evidence is however another matter and this is explored further below.

Another stimulus to the growing interest in project portfolio management has come from the perception of continuing failure in project and programme delivery and benefits realisation. The Public Accounts Committee commented in 1999 that[11] *'for more than two decades, implementing IT systems successfully has proved difficult...implementation of IT systems has resulted in delay, confusion and inconvenience to the citizen and, in many cases, poor value for money to the taxpayer'.* A study of large public sector projects for HM Treasury by Mott MacDonald in 2002 found a *'high level of optimism in project estimates arising from underestimating project costs and duration or overestimating project benefits'.*[12] The OGC[13] has estimated that *'30–40 per cent of systems to support business change deliver no benefits whatsoever'* and a publication from the Major Projects Association refers to the *'calamitous history of previous cost overruns of very large projects in the public sector'.*[14] One leading academic in the project management arena comments, *'The recent reports from the United Kingdom National Audit Office confirms that in spite of all the changes in project management, there has been no improvement in performance. The US General Accounting Office reported a similar outcome.'*[15]

This issue is not peculiar to the public sector. A report in 2004 for the Royal Academy of Engineering and the British Computer Society[16] found little difference between public and private sectors and concluded: *'It is alarming that significant numbers of complex software and IT projects still fail to deliver key benefits on time and to target cost and specification.'* It also referred to a study carried out by Oxford University and *Computer Weekly* which found that only 16 per cent of IT projects were considered successful.[17]

---

11 Public Accounts Committee of the House of Commons (1999) *Improving the Delivery of Government IT Projects*, Available at: http://www.publications.parliament.uk/pa/cm199900/cmselect/cmpubacc/65/6502.htm [Last accessed: 1ˢᵗ December 2008].

12 Mott MacDonald (2002) *Review of Large Public Procurement in the UK*, Available at: http://www.hm-treasury.gov.uk/d/7(3).pdf [Last accessed: 1st December 2008].

13 OGC Successful Delivery Toolkit (2005) quoted at http://www.bcs.org/server.php?show=ConWebDoc.16425.

14 Quoted by Flyvbjerg, B. et al. (2007) in *Megaprojects and Risk. An Anatomy of Ambition*, Cambridge University Press, Cambridge, p. 4.

15 Dombkins, D. (2009) 'Redefining Our Profession Part 2: The History and Future of Project Management', *PM World Today*, February 2009, XI:II.

16 Royal Academy of Engineering (April 2004) *The Challenges of Complex IT Projects, The report of a working group from the Royal Academy of Engineering and The British Computer Society.*

17 Sauer, C. and Cuthbertson, C. (November 2003) *The State of IT Project Management in the UK*, Templeton College, Oxford.

Nor is this a UK phenomenon – a study by the Standish Group (2004)[18] reported average cost escalation on IT projects of 43 per cent, and 71 per cent of projects were late, over budget and under scope. The HM Treasury Green Book[19] concludes that optimism bias in cost and benefit forecasts is a '*world-wide phenomenon that affects both the private and public sectors*' and KPMG reported in their 2005 global IT survey that '*project success appears to equate to achieving an acceptable level of failure or minimizing lost benefits*'.[20]

Such failings have been attributed, at least in part, to the absence of portfolio management processes and techniques. Kendall and Rollins (2003)[21] for example, argue that four generic problems are associated with the absence of project portfolio management: too many projects; projects that do not add value; projects that are not linked to strategic goals; and an unbalanced portfolio. The CFO Executive Board estimate[22] that 40 per cent of incremental expansions and 90 per cent of discontinuous innovations fail to achieve their predicted growth and profitability targets and a primary root cause of this was politicised decision making. Gartner similarly report[23] that organisations without stringent risk assessment processes will cancel more than 20 per cent of projects in the execution phase and Giga Information Group estimate that organisations waste between 5 and 8 per cent of their entire IT spend due to duplicated, unaligned and ineffective projects.[24]

It is this context of, on the one hand, a perception of continuing project and programme failure in terms of delivery and benefits realisation, and on the other, the claimed potential benefits of project portfolio management, that have led to increasing calls for the application of 'best practice' project portfolio management to ensure:

---

18 Standish Group (2004) *CHAOS report*. Cited on http://en.wikipedia.org/wiki/Cost_overrun [Last accessed: 13th December 2008].

19 HM Treasury (2003) *The Green Book Appraisal and Evaluation in Central Government*, TSO, London.

20 KPMG (2005) Global IT Project Management Survey.

21 Kendall, G. and Rollins, S. (2003) *Advanced Project Portfolio Management and the PMO*, J. Ross Publishing, Florida, Quoted in Reyck et al. (2005).

22 CFO Executive Board (July 2004) *Disciplined Capital Budgeting Aligning Investment Proposals with Enterprise Strategy*. Cited in Sanwal, A. (2007) *Optimizing Corporate Portfolio Management*, John Wiley, Hoboken, New Jersey.

23 Quoted in *Project Portfolio Management: Maximising Enterprise Investments*, April 2003, BusinessEngine White Paper.

24 Giga Information Group Planning Assumption, *Maximising IT Value: Portfolio Management Options for 2003*, Murphy, P., Gliedman, C. and Visitacion, M. January 6th 2003, quoted in '*Project Portfolio Management: Maximising Enterprise Investments*, April 2003, BusinessEngine White Paper.

- more of the 'right' projects and programmes are undertaken in terms of greater financial benefits and contribution to strategic targets and business priorities, and fewer 'wrong' ones are started or are killed off earlier, via active management of the project portfolio;

- removal of redundant and duplicate projects when the portfolio is examined from an enterprise-wide perspective;

- more effective implementation of projects and programmes via management of the project pipeline, project dependencies, inter-dependencies and constraints (including resources, skills, infrastructure and change 'appetite' or capacity) and redirecting funding when projects do not deliver, or are no longer strategically aligned;

- more efficient utilisation of scarce resources including skilled project managers – the scope for improvement here has been highlighted in research for CA[25] which finds that the main criterion for assigning staff to projects is availability rather than suitability;

- greater benefits realisation via active approaches to the exploitation of capacity and capability created; and

- improved accountability and corporate governance.

If this is true, the potential benefits are indeed significant and the remainder of this chapter examines the evidence that underlies the claims outlined above, that is, what evidence is there that application of a portfolio management approach has *in practice* led to improved performance? But first, some observations on the likelihood of such evidence being available.

Potential Issues in Demonstrating the Case for Project Portfolio Management

One might suppose that organisations would be reluctant to publicise the results of their implementations of portfolio management – publicly admitting failure might damage stakeholder confidence and revealing the sources of success might, particularly in the private sector, be seen as giving away a source of competitive advantage. In addition to this, there are several reasons why it might

---

25 Loudhouse Research (2008) *The Changing Face of Project Management*.

be anticipated that there would be limited hard empirical evidence to demonstrate the impact of project portfolio management, including: the current general degree of maturity in the practical application of project portfolio management; methodological difficulties in measuring its impact; and the assumed strength of the normative case outlined above (the case just seems so self-evident), which can act as a disincentive to formal evaluation of the business case for project portfolio management. These factors are reviewed briefly below.

Firstly, it is still early days in applying portfolio management in the project environment – to the extent that it has been adopted, many organisations are at the early stages of implementation. OGC guidance[26] states that: *'It is important to note that Portfolio Management is an immature delivery practice in government.'* The I&DeA website paints a similar picture in relation to local government:[27] *'Unlike project and programme management, there isn't a de facto standard for project portfolio management, and in local authorities the practice and experience is relatively new.'* A similar picture has been found in other jurisdictions and in the private sector. Application of the Information Technology Investment Management (ITIM) framework used by the US General Accounting Office (GAO) has found that most organisations reviewed were operating at Stage 2 ('Building the Investment Foundation') out of five. Also in the IT field, Gartner have reported that project portfolio management is a relatively immature discipline with most large organisations ranking their maturity level as low to medium.[28] A meeting of Government CIO's from four European countries in 2007[29] reported that whilst progress was being made in demonstrating the public value of IT, in terms of business case development and benefits management, what was missing was a process to connect the two: *'None of the participants said they have a portfolio management process that requires individual projects to update their benefit and risk profiles during the implementation phase.'* The Gartner paper concluded that: *'Government CIOs and program managers must start focusing more on portfolio management to maintain alignment between business and IT throughout the life cycles of their projects.'*

Consequently few organisations can be expected to have reached a level of maturity where overall portfolio progress and impact on organisational performance can be evaluated formally.

---

26 OGC (May 2004) *Portfolio Management* Version 1.0.
27 http://www.idea.gov.uk/idk/core/page.do?pageId=5829740 [Last accessed: 18th January 2008].
28 Gomolski, B. and Smith, M. (27 November 2006) *Program and Portfolio Management: Getting to the Next Level*, Gartner ID Number: G00144601.
29 Di Maio, A. (2007) *Findings: Many Understand the Public Value of IT, but Few Act on It*, Gartner ID number: G00152239.

Secondly, there are what Pollitt (1995)[30] refers to as '*fundamental epistemological and methodological issues*' in attributing performance improvements to one specific factor. We may implement a new process but it is rarely possible to say with certainty that the initiative is responsible for any subsequent performance changes. As Pollitt and Bouckaert (2000)[31] say, '*The availability of such outcome measures confidently linked to programme interventions, is the exception rather than the rule.*' Problems with outcome measurement and attribution are compounded by the fact that even if we can show that certain changes in outcome are correlated with specified input/process changes, this does not demonstrate causation – performance improvement may be due to some other factor[32] or the relationship could be the reverse of that proposed and '*the "arrow of causation"*' may be the opposite of that assumed, that is, improved project delivery may lead to the adoption of a portfolio management approach rather than vice versa. Thus measuring the impact of portfolio management is problematic because many of the benefits will be non-financial (although they may well ultimately contribute to improved financial outcomes) or difficult to measure (what is the value of poor projects that are not started for example?) or to attribute to the application of portfolio management rather than improved project and programme management or indeed to routine management practice.

Beyond problems with the relative immaturity of project portfolio management practices and measurement, there is another reason to believe that empirical evidence of the impact of portfolio management might be short on the ground, particularly in the public sector. Pollitt has identified a paradox at the heart of what is termed 'New Public Management'[33] in that despite the emphasis on evaluation (and the belief that interventions should be 'evidence-based') such approaches/frameworks have not themselves been subjected to serious and systematic evaluation. Pollitt concluded that, '*Support for the NPM package as a whole is based more on faith and doctrine than on demonstrable track record.*' Pollitt and Bouckaert (2000) comment that, '*The vocabulary of management reform carries a definite normative "charge"*' and that progress is often equated with implementation

---

30 Pollitt, C. (1995) 'Justification by Works or by Faith? Evaluating the New Public Management', *Evaluation*, 1:2, October, pp. 133–154.

31 Pollitt, C. and Bouckaert, G. (2000) *Public Management Reform, A Comparative Analysis*, Oxford University Press, Oxford.

32 For example, as was demonstrated by Elton Mayo and the Hawthorne Experiments.

33 '*New Public Management (NPM) is a management philosophy used by governments since the 1980s to modernise the public sector. NPM is a broad and very complex term used to describe the wave of public sector reforms throughout the world since the 1980s. Based on public choice and managerial schools of thought, NPM seeks to enhance the efficiency of the public sector and the control that government has over it. The main hypothesis in the NPM-reform wave is that more market orientation in the public sector will lead to greater cost-efficiency for governments, without having negative side effects on other objectives and considerations*'. Source: Wikipedia http://en.wikipedia.org/wiki/New_Public_Management.

of process rather than impact.[34] They note however that the NPM claims are not based on empirical evidence and refer to '*the paucity of any scientific basis for the knowledge which they're (implicitly or explicitly) claiming to convey*'.

So, for several reasons, one might expect to find limited empirical evidence supporting the case for project portfolio management – and that which does exist could be expected to be more qualitative than quantitative in nature. Whether this is the case, or whether a more substantive case can be made for the application of portfolio management to the change agenda is explored further in the remainder of this chapter.

The Evidence for Project Portfolio Management

What we have seen above is that there is a prima facie, theoretical case for undertaking project portfolio management in ensuring a more strategically aligned, balanced and achievable change programme. In addition, the introduction of rigorous and consistent approaches to investment appraisal, portfolio prioritisation and project performance management clearly have benefits in demonstrating adherence to corporate governance requirements in terms of transparency about the investment justification, and accountability for delivery and benefits realisation.[35] But what evidence is there that demonstrates project portfolio management has a payback, however this is defined and measured, *in practice*?

Much of the research on the impact of project portfolio management has been undertaken in the areas of Information Technology and New Product Development. The evidence from these areas is reviewed first before we examine four short case studies from the public and private sectors here in the UK and abroad.

The Application of Project Portfolio Management to Information Technology

Industry research organisations such as Gartner, Forrester and Butler Group report cost savings from applying project portfolio management in the order

---

34 In this regard, note the findings reported in Chapter 8 concerning the absence of any robust evaluation of most of the project portfolio maturity frameworks.

35 For example, note the contribution of project portfolio management to the CPA assessment noted in the Cambridgeshire County Council case study on page 15.

of 10–20 per cent of the total IT budget – but are such reports supported by reliable research?

Researchers from London and Ashridge Business Schools[36] undertook a study in 2005 that sought to assess the correlation between the application of project portfolio management processes and techniques, and improvements in project performance. They used an approach similar to that used by Ibbs and Regato[37] in demonstrating a positive relationship between project management maturity and improvements in cost and schedule performance. The study was based on a survey questionnaire of 125 medium to large size companies from the UK, Europe and the rest of the world. The researchers reported a strong correlation between increasing adoption of project portfolio management processes and a reduction in project-related problems as well as project performance, that is, portfolio management was seen to be correlated with improved project performance and this link increases with the maturity of the processes adopted. The researchers concluded that, *'This means that as organizations increasingly adopt PPM approaches, the impact is strengthened.'*

Weill and Ross (2004) report that a Massachusetts Institute of Technology (MIT) study of more than 300 organisations in 23 countries found growth and agility was linked to a portfolio approach. They also argue that governance is crucial and that organisations *'with superior IT governance have more than 20% higher profit than firms with poor governance given the same strategic objectives'*.[38] Research by Weill and Woodham (2002)[39] similarly found that an effective governance structure is the most important predictor of getting value from IT. The importance of governance in project portfolio management is explored further in Chapter 7.

In another MIT study, Jeffery and Leliveld (2004)[40] surveyed 130 Fortune 100 CIOs and undertook selected in-depth interviews. They found that 65

36 Reyck, B. D., Grushka-Cockayne, Y. D., Lockett, M., Calderini, S. R., Moura, M. and Sloper, A. (February 2005) 'The Impact of Project Portfolio Management on Information Technology Projects', *International Journal of Project Management* 23:7, pp. 524–537.
37 Ibbs, W. and Regato, J. (2002) *Quantifying the Value of Project Management*, PMI, Newton Square, PA.
38 Weill, P. and Ross, J. (2004) *IT Governance: How Top Performers Manage IT Decision Rights for Superior Results*, Harvard Business School Publishing, Boston, Mass.
39 Weill, P. and Woodham, R. (2002) *Don't Just Lead, Govern: Implementing Effective IT Governance*, MIT Sloan, Center for Information Systems Research (CISR), Working Paper #326, April.
40 Jeffery, M. and Leliveld, I. (2004) 'Best Practices in IT Portfolio Management', *MIT Sloan Management Review*, Spring, 45: 3, pp. 41–49

per cent believed IT project portfolio management yields significant business value, although only 17 per cent appeared to be realising the potential value in practice. Based on their research, Jeffery and Leliveld propose an IT portfolio management maturity model based on four levels – ad hoc, defined, managed and synchronised. The distribution of organisations across the levels was reported to be: ad hoc 4.5 per cent, defined 24.5 per cent, managed 54 per cent and synchronised 17 per cent. Jeffery and Leliveld argued that only enterprises at the synchronised stage show a link between portfolio management and improved return on asset performance. The benefits of this level of maturity were however substantial – those at the synchronised level achieved cost savings of 40 per cent, better alignment of IT budgets and business strategy, and greater central coordination of IT investments across the organisation. Other benefits identified by interviewees included: wider support from senior business management; the process was perceived to be fair and objective; and it resulted in increased investment in IT.

Others have claimed significant benefits from achieving even basic levels of portfolio management maturity – from removal of low value, duplicate, redundant and poorly performing projects. CIO Magazine[41] for example, report that just compiling an IT portfolio database saved one company $3m and another $4.5m from identifying redundancies. In another study, Verhoef[42] from the Department of Mathematics and Computer Science at the Free University of Amsterdam, noted that in one organisation with a $500m IT portfolio, direct cost savings were 3–5 per cent per annum of the total portfolio value from better decision making, killing poorly performing projects and those with a negative return on investment, mitigating risks, and removing redundancies.

The Application of Project Portfolio Management to New Product Development

A 2005 Bain study of the Global Innovation 1000[43] found no relationship between the scale of research and development spend and economic success, although it concluded that insufficient spending could damage organisational health. Rather than the scale of investment, the 'difference that made the difference'

41 Berinato, S. (2001) 'Do the Math', *CIO Magazine*. October.
42 Verhoef, C. *Quantitative IT Portfolio Management*, Available at: http://www.cs.vu.nl/~x/ipm/ipm. pdf [Last Accessed: 14th December 2008].
43 Quoted in Sanwal, A. (2007) *Optimizing Corporate Portfolio Management*, John Wiley, Hoboken, New Jersey.

was the quality of the innovation process – in short, the process that determines which projects are undertaken and how they are managed.

Robert Cooper, Professor at McMaster University in Canada, has researched and written extensively on the subjects of New Product Development and innovation – and he reaches similar conclusions to the Bain study. One benchmarking study undertaken with the American Productivity & Quality Centre concluded,[44] *'Exceptional performance in product development is no accident. Rather it is the result of a disciplined, systematic approach based on best practices.'* In short, organisations that adopt these practices were found to consistently outperform the rest. Cooper asserts that, *'Numerous studies have confirmed that there is no direct link between a company's increase in spending in R&D and their success rate with new products. What then, if not spending, drives new product success? Significant productivity gains (in NPD) are possible through astute project selection. In fact, top performing businesses are four times more likely to deploy such practices, namely effective portfolio management.'*[45]

Tetrapak[46] is a multinational food processing and packaging company. They have identified the following benefits derived from prioritisation of the product portfolio, and actions taken to strengthen the product portfolio from a product value perspective:

- improved efficiency in the creation of new products;

- resources focused on the 'right' projects – all activities (cross-functional and cross-organisational) are linked and aligned to agreed strategies;

- more 'right' products were created and delivered – product strategies were aligned across product categories and markets; and

- more value for R&D invested money.

Demonstrable impacts included: projects delivered on time and sales of new products increased significantly.

---

44 *Winning at New Products: Pathways to Profitable Innovation,* Available at: http://www.stage-gate. com/downloads/Winning_at_New_Products_Pathways_to_Profitable_Innovation.pdf   [Last accessed: 13th December 2008].

45 Marketing materials for a seminar: Developing a Product Innovation Strategy and Deciding your new product portfolio Making Strategic Choices and Picking the Winners, March 2008.

46 Sourced from correspondence between Stephen Jenner and Bengt Nilsson, Tetrapak, July 2007 and February 2008.

A review of the literature and empirical evidence by Killen et al. (2007) in Australia[47] noted that whilst portfolio management maturity was low, there was some evidence that more formal processes lead to improved outcomes. A recent survey undertaken by the same researchers[48] of 60 Australian organisations came to similar conclusions to those of Cooper at al. in the US[49] – New Product Development '*success is twice as likely in organizations that are 'top' PPM performers than in 'poor' PPM performers*' (where PPM refers to Project Portfolio Management).

EXAMPLE 1.   MAKING THE CASE FOR PORTFOLIO MANAGEMENT: THE CRIMINAL JUSTICE SYSTEM IT PORTFOLIO

CJS IT was a £2 billion investment between 2003 and 2008 in modernising IT infrastructure, implementing modern case management systems, and joining them up to facilitate information sharing across the criminal justice system. A portfolio management approach was implemented in early 2005 to address problems of project slippage, cost escalation and low levels of quantified benefits. The impact of the approach adopted was seen in significant improvements in project delivery and cost containment so freeing up funds for additional investments including those in the youth justice system which accounts for 25 per cent of all criminal cases. Booked benefits increased from £853m to £2.6 billion. The regimes adopted helped restore the confidence of HM Treasury and contributed to the funding baseline being maintained across three spending review periods at a time when many other budgets were being cut.

The approach was independently recognised in reports to the OECD[1] and European Commission[2] and won the 2007 Civil Service Financial Management award. Booz Allen Hamilton[3] reported in an international e-government benchmarking study on '*sound investment practices...CJIT has adopted many best-practice investment tools...recognized by the EC as a leader in this field in Europe*', and Gartner[4]

1   Cabinet Office (2006) Report to the OECD on the UK Approach to Benefits Realisation.
2   Economics of eGovernment Project (2006) *Compendium to the Measurement Framework*, Available at: http://www.umic.pt/images/stories/publicacoes200709/Measurement_Framework_Compendium.pdf.
3   Booz Allen Hamilton (2005) *International e-Gov Benchmarking Study*.
4   Di Maio, A. (2005) *UK Criminal Justice System Makes Portfolio Management Key to IT Success*, Gartner ID Number: G00130564.

---

47   Killen, C. P., Hunt, R. A. and Kleinschmidt, E. J. (2007) *Managing the New Product Development Project Portfolio: A Review of the Literature and Empirical Evidence*, Proceedings of Portland International Conference on Managing Engineering and Technology (PICMET) 2007, Portland, Oregon.
48   Killen, C. P., Hunt, R. A. and Kleinschmidt, E. J. (2008) 'Project Portfolio Management for Product Innovation', *International Journal of Quality and Reliability Management*, 25:1, pp 24–38.
49   Cooper, R. G., Edgett, S. J. and Kleinschmidt, E. J. (2001) *Portfolio Management for New Products*, 2nd ed, Perseus Press, Cambridge Mass.

concluded that, *'The facilitating role of the IT portfolio unit represent good practices. Government organizations that are seeking successful approaches to program and project portfolio management should study CJIT's actions.'*

EXAMPLE 2.   MAKING THE CASE FOR PORTFOLIO MANAGEMENT: CAMBRIDGESHIRE COUNTY COUNCIL

A study into successful IT-enabled business change projects by the National Audit Office[1] included review of the approach to project portfolio management applied at Cambridgeshire County Council. The NAO concluded that the benefits realised included:

- more cross cutting initiatives undertaken by overcoming functional silos and directing resources to those initiatives most aligned with business priorities;
- viewing activities as a single portfolio provides management with 'the whole picture';
- weaker business cases are rejected earlier;
- efficiency savings from better management of the Authority's financial and human resources and strategic risks; and
- it supports the Comprehensive Performance Assessment (CPA) process.

Cambridgeshire's analysis concludes, *'It is still early days but there is evidence of more rational decision-making as a result of developing some PPfM tools and techniques. More accessible, timely and accurate information is also improving the quality of decision-making.'*[2]

---

1   National Audit Office (17th November 2006) *Delivering Successful IT-enabled Business Change*, Available at: http://www.nao.org.uk/publications/0607/delivering_successful_it-enabl.aspx [Last accessed: 13th December 2008].
2   *Project Portfolio Management Framework*, Cambridgeshire County Council, Available at: www.idea.gov.uk/idk/core/page.do?pageId=5829740 [Last accessed: 13th December 2008].

EXAMPLE 3.   MAKING THE CASE FOR PORTFOLIO MANAGEMENT: QUEENSLAND UNIVERSITY OF TECHNOLOGY

According to Warren Fraser, Project Portfolio Manager from 2000 to 2007, the impact of portfolio management can be seen in:[1]

- The level of investment as a proxy for organisation confidence: prior to establishment of the Portfolio Project Office (PPO), the University had a number of disjointed funding mechanisms. At the establishment of the

---

1   This information was sourced from correspondence between Stephen Jenner and Warren Fraser (Associate Director, IT Services) in February 2008.

PPO, these were combined into a central pool with governance processes supported by the PPO. Investment increased more than three-fold from 2000 to 2007.

- Project benefits articulation and realisation improved with explicit review both prior to funding (ex ante) and ex post via post implementation reviews.
- Favourable comments both by the Internal Audit Office and the State Audit Office.
- Project Management rigour improved due to the explicit and enforced connection between funding and compliance with portfolio processes and governance.

EXAMPLE 4.   MAKING THE CASE FOR PORTFOLIO MANAGEMENT: AMERICAN EXPRESS

Anand Sanwal details the approach to investment optimisation developed at American Express in his book *Optimizing Corporate Portfolio Management*,[1] Sanwal argues for the application of portfolio management to all discretionary spend and claims that it: helped breakdown silos and provided an objective means to allocate resources; as a dynamic process it facilitated organisational flexibility; and enhanced transparency helped create internal competition for investment ideas and ultimately funding. He also points to the following specific indicators of success:

- Recognition by winning the Baseline Magazine Award grand prize and prize for innovation. Whilst the prize was for the software solution, Sanwal argues that the real source of value add was not the software but the disciplined process that made different projects and investments comparable as well as the efforts made to address behavioral and cultural issues so they could depoliticise decision-making. The company's efforts have also been recognised by CFO magazine, the CFO Executive Board and InfoWorld.
- The approach has been cited by Wall Street analysts as enabling resource allocation flexibility. Sanwal argues that this is a main contributory factor behind AmEx commanding a premium price to earnings ratio valuation relative to their competitors.
- The Corporate Portfolio Management (CPM) effort has facilitated major strategic shifts – for example, in October 2005, they exited a major business, American Express Financial Advisors, because the CPM process revealed that the business couldn't compete for investment funding versus its card business because of its risk-reward characteristics. As a result, it made more sense for this business to be separate so it could grow.

---

1   Sourced from Sanwal, A. (2007) *Optimizing Corporate Portfolio Management,* and from subsequent correspondence and meetings with the author.

- They also utilised CPM data to review investment time horizons to see if they had an appropriate balance of short, medium and long-term investments. The result was reallocation of funds and the creation of a $50 million Innovation Fund to seed longer-term, disruptive ideas. For these efforts, *Fortune* Magazine named American Express the most innovative company in banking and credit cards.
- In 2006 they reallocated tens of million of dollars across business division lines. Given the entrenched silos that often develop in large, complex organisations, this was regarded as a major success for the process and the first time such reallocations had occurred in the history of the organisation.
- A significant endorsement for the CPM effort came when Gary Crittenden left to become the CFO/COO of Citigroup – at a meeting with Wall Street analysts he declared his first objective was to bring CPM to Citigroup.

Chapter 1 Conclusions and Take-aways

1. There is a strong theoretical case for using project portfolio management to improve prioritisation of initiatives against organisational priorities, maintain strategic alignment and effectively manage constraints and dependencies across the whole collection of change projects, programmes and initiatives.

2. Notwithstanding issues in measurement and the limited maturity of portfolio management practices, this theoretical case is supported by research evidence in the UK, US and Australia (Reyck et al., Jeffery and Leliveld, Cooper, Killen and so on) and case studies that demonstrate that portfolio management can reduce costs, enable performance improvements and reduce risk.

3. Depending on the current organisational position, significant benefits are available from achieving basic levels of project portfolio management maturity – establishing an enterprise-wide view of all project activity can deliver substantial financial benefits from removal of redundant, duplicate and poorly performing projects and from gaining an insight into how investments in one part of the organisation can be leveraged elsewhere. In addition, such organisations are better able to demonstrate effective stewardship of public resources and adherence to corporate governance requirements.

4. Additional benefits are linked with increasing process maturity and active management of the portfolio, but such benefits are often

more difficult to measure in financial terms since they relate to factors such as improved strategic alignment and a more balanced portfolio in terms of risk exposure, product life cycle stage and alignment with the organisations' capacity to absorb change.

5.   As we shall see later in the book, the highest levels of maturity represent a changed mindset in which: the focus of attention doesn't end with implementation but when benefits are realised; project and asset portfolios are proactively managed; and learning from previous projects is fed back into the investment selection and portfolio management processes. We now turn to consideration of how these potential benefits can be realised.

2

The Prerequisites for Success

'And what is good, Phaedrus, and what is not good – need we ask anyone to tell us these things?'

Plato, The Phaedrus

> After reading this chapter you will:
> - be aware of the four prerequisites for successful implementation of project portfolio management;
> - understand why two factors that are often cited as being crucial are in fact, not required.

Introduction

Chapter 1 demonstrated that there is a body of quantitative and qualitative evidence that is supportive of the hypothesis that project portfolio management has significant potential organisational benefits. Whilst recognising these potential benefits, many organisations struggle to implement portfolio management effectively – they are unsure about where to begin, how to sustain progress in the medium to longer term, and how to ensure their efforts amount to more than just another layer of bureaucracy. So whilst Plato may have suggested that in the field of metaphysics the answer to the question, *'what is good?'* lies within ourselves, when it comes to project portfolio management it is instructive to look at what has worked elsewhere. This chapter therefore takes the next step in identifying the prerequisites for effective project portfolio management. This lays the basis for consideration of portfolio management processes in more detail in Chapters 3–6.

The portfolio management guidance issued by the OGC in 2004 identified three prerequisites that need to be in place in order to successfully implement project portfolio management. The first of these is, *'Organisational capability in Programme and Project Management (PPM) governance and standards.'*[1] The implications of this view are that an organisation should not attempt to establish portfolio management until it has achieved a relatively mature state in relation to project and programme management. This view was reflected in advice from consultants on the application of the original version of the OGC's P3M3 Maturity Model which saw portfolio management building on existing project and programme management maturity – *'This means that organizations can use the model to evolve their maturity across all disciplines in an integrated approach or by addressing Project Management then Programme Management and then Portfolio Management in sequence.'*[2] Venning[3] (2008) emphasises the point when he says that the prerequisites of portfolio management include, *'Organizational capability in programme and project management with consistent standards'* and *'organizations should not attempt to establish a portfolio management function until they are confident that they have reached an appropriate level of maturity in their programme and project management approaches. The minimum recommended level is Level 3 of the OGC's P3M3.'*

The problem we immediately face is that one of the explanations for the absence of formal evaluation of the popular maturity models, including P3M3, is the relatively low level of maturity reached by most organisations reviewed. If we accept this analysis, then most organisations should not even consider project portfolio management; but this is illogical and furthermore it rests on a misunderstanding of the nature of project portfolio management. Firstly, the consequence of the above view is that an organisation needs to develop its capability to deliver projects irrespective of their business value before asking the question are they the right projects to undertake in the first place – so putting the 'delivery cart' before the 'strategy horse'. Secondly, portfolio management calls for a different set of competencies and disciplines from project and programme management. Whilst the latter involves detailed planning and a focus on managing implementation, portfolio management core competencies relate more to the disciplines of business strategy, finance and economics – in deciding what projects to undertake, where to continue to invest and how to optimise value from the investment made. A study of

---

1   The others were: Top management commitment and organisational willingness to implement new processes.

2   Outperform, *Capability Maturity Models – Using P3M3 to Improve Performance*, Available at: http://www.outperform.co.uk/Portals/0/P3M3%20Performance%20Improvement%201v2-APP. pdf [Last accessed: 13th December 2008].

3   Venning, C. (2007) *Managing Portfolios of Change with MSP from programmes and PRINCE2 for projects*, TSO, London.

lessons learned in applying portfolio management to Information Technology in the US Government[4] concluded that 'Lesson Number 1' was: '*Understand the differences and the relationship between portfolio management and project management and manage each one accordingly.*' The latest guidance from the OGC[5] agrees that project portfolio management is not dependent on effective project and programme management. Let's be clear, the two disciplines are related, but project portfolio management is *not* Über-project or programme management.

Consequently, whilst effective project and programme management plays a crucial role in addressing the delivery issue of 'doing projects right', ultimately portfolio management also addresses the wider questions of: '*are we doing the right projects and programmes*' (in terms of our strategic priorities), '*are they achievable*' individually and collectively, and '*are we realising the potential benefits*'? Seen from this perspective, project portfolio management can add value irrespective of the degree of organisational maturity in project and programme management.

Another commonly cited prerequisite of effective portfolio management is the use of a software tool. There is no doubt that popular packages such as Clarity, ProSight, Planview and Microsoft Project Portfolio Server offer advantages including: providing a central repository for project data; resource scheduling; and data analysis and reporting. These advantages are particularly noticeable in portfolios with a large number of projects and programmes. Practical experience however shows that repeatable processes and effective governance come first – software tools should normally be considered once these are in place and the tool should be adapted to organisational processes not vice versa. Research by Reyck et al. (2005)[6] from London and Ashridge Business Schools concluded that software is '*only justifiable when the other aspects of PPM are already in place*'. Sanwal[7] comes to a similar conclusion: '*Technology, thoughtfully applied, can help you enable the process with greater efficiency, accountability, and transparency, but it is not the solution or even one of the most essential components of the solution.*' He

---

4　The Best Practices Committee of the Federal CIO Council (March 2002) *Summary of First Practices and Lessons Learned in Information Technology Portfolio Management*, Available at: http://www.cio.gov/documents/BPC_portfolio_final.pdf [Last accessed: 14th December 2008].

5　This guidance includes the revised version of P3M3 maturity framework and '*Portfolio Management Guide*' which is currently (March 2009) at public consultation draft stage.

6　Reyck, B. D., Grushka-Cockayne, Y., Lockett, M., Calderini, S. R., Moura, M. and Sloper, A. (2005) 'The Impact of Project Portfolio Management on Information Technology Projects', *International Journal of Project Management*, 23: February, pp. 524–537.

7　Sanwal, A. (2007) *Optimizing Corporate Portfolio Management*, John Wiley, Hoboken, New Jersey.

also quotes Gartner analyst Matt Light at the Gartner Symposium/ITxpo 2006 as saying, '*A fool with a tool is still a fool.*'

If project and programme management maturity and software solutions are not prerequisites for project portfolio management success what are? A review of the literature by Reyck et al. (2005)[8] found that three preconditions underpin the successful implementation of project portfolio management:

1. a clear organisational strategy against which the portfolio can be aligned;

2. top management support to overcome silo mentalities and aid resource re-allocation; and

3. team skills – those responsible for operating the process need to be suitably skilled in both finance and business strategy.

Whilst this analysis related to the IT project portfolio, these factors are also relevant to the wider enterprise business change portfolio. We examine each of these prerequisites in a little more detail below.

A Clearly Articulated Organisational Strategy

At its most basic, portfolio management seeks to ensure that our investment in projects and programmes are aligned with organisational strategy and business priorities. It therefore follows that these strategies and priorities need to be clearly articulated if we are to use them as a basis for prioritising actual and potential investments.

Brian Quinn famously said, '*A good deal of corporate planning … is like a ritual rain dance. It has no effect on the weather that follows, but those who engage in it think it does. … Moreover, much of the advice related to corporate planning is directed at improving the dancing, not the weather.*'[9]

---

8   Reyck, B. D., Grushka-Cockayne, Y., Lockett, M., Calderini, S. R., Moura, M. and Sloper, A., (2005) 'The Impact of Project Portfolio Management on Information Technology Projects', *International Journal of Project Management*, 23: February 2005, pp. 524–537.

9   Quoted by Peters, T. at http://www.johnldavidson.com/tompeters.pdf [Last accessed: 14th December 2008].

The point is that all organisations have a project portfolio and a strategy in the sense that where they spend their resources reflects their portfolio and strategy in practice. The issue is linking the two, that is, relating the resource allocation process to strategic targets and business priorities, and maintaining this linkage in the context of changing conditions. This linkage is not always obvious – the NAO/OGC's 'Agreed List of Common Causes of failure in IT-enabled projects' includes the following at number 1 – '*Lack of clear link between the project and the organisation's key strategic priorities including agreed measures of success.*'

Making this link requires that strategy is clearly articulated – for example, the UK Government's Capability Review asks, '*Do you have a clear, coherent and achievable strategy with a single, overarching set of challenging outcomes, aims, objectives and success measures?*' Where this is the case, we then have a basis for assessing projects' strategic contribution. Techniques that facilitate this are discussed in Chapter 4, but one technique which I call 'Strategic Contribution Analysis' combines clearly articulated strategy with benefits mapping to provide a clear line of sight from strategy to initiative (and vice versa), and in turn to individual performance objectives, that is, an analysis of the investment logic chain that combines:

- Strategy Mapping – from Vision (where we are trying to get) through Strategy (how we will get there) to Success measures (how we'll know we've arrived successfully); with

- Benefits Mapping (such as shown in Example 14 in Chapter 4) – demonstrating how investment in change initiatives results in benefits and the contribution of these benefits to the success measures referred to above.

An example of a Strategy Map drawn up from the UK Government's Service Transformation Agreement is shown in Figure 2.1.[10]

In this way we have a clear statement of the objectives or vision of a strategy, how it will be achieved, and what the agreed measures of success are. We then have a basis for strategy-led resource allocation by consistently assessing the contribution of projects to our agreed measures of strategic success – at

---

10 This Strategy Map was compiled by the author from the HM Government (2007) *Service Transformation Agreement,* Available at: http://www.hm-treasury.gov.uk/d/pbr_csr07_service.pdf [Last accessed: 1st December 2008].

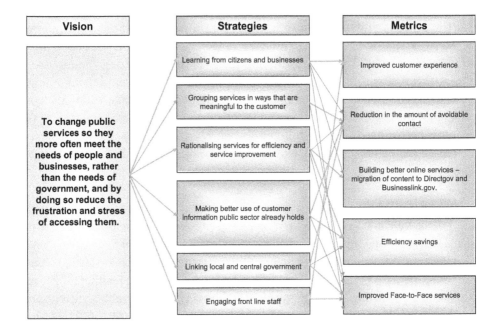

Figure 2.1   Strategy map for the Service Transformation Agreement

which point we can start, in Brian Quinn's terms, to 'influence the weather' by determining:

- that all initiatives are *necessary* for the achievement of the measures of strategic success; and

- that collectively, the portfolio is *sufficient* to achieve the strategic targets.

It should also be noted that when portfolio management is implemented, the relationship between strategy and resource allocation often becomes a two-way process rather than the top-down process usually envisaged[11] – strategy itself is, as Mintzberg has noted,[12] emergent, and as such is informed by the

---

11 For example, see Killen, C. P., Hunt, R. A. and Kleinschmidt, E. J. (2007) *Managing the New Product Development Project Portfolio: A Review of the Literature and Empirical Evidence*, Proceedings of PICMET 2007 Portland, Oregon, Portland International Conference on Managing Engineering and Technology (PICMET) and Killen, C. P., Hunt, R. A. and Kleinschmidt, E. J. (2008) 'Project Portfolio Management for Product Innovation', *International Journal of Quality and Reliability Management*, 25:1, pp. 24–38.

12 Mintzberg, H. (1994) *The Rise and Fall of Strategic Planning*, Prentice Hall, UK.

results of analysing forecast contribution as well as evaluating previous investments.

Top Management Support

The NAO[13] in their 2006 study of successful IT-enabled business change, concluded that senior level engagement is crucial to successful delivery in three ways:

1. By providing mechanisms to prioritise the project portfolio in line with business objectives, ensuring there is the capacity to support them and that the portfolio represents the optimum balance between benefits and risk.

2. By creating a clear decision-making structure, with agreed lines of accountability, so that the right decisions are made swiftly and in line with business strategy.

3. By demonstrating that senior management is committed to the change.

Ultimately portfolio management is an enterprise-level activity that cuts across business unit objectives in favour of organisation-wide priorities. Commitment from the very highest levels is therefore required if business unit heads are to leave their silo hats outside the room when resource allocation decisions are made.

EXAMPLE 5.   THE IMPORTANCE OF A SENIOR SPONSOR

A key factor in the successful implementation of a portfolio management approach to the CJS IT programme across three departments and seven criminal justice organisations, was the commitment of the Director General and support of HM Treasury. This was regarded as crucial in making progress in a short period of time, forcing through decisions and preventing the initiative from becoming bogged down in arguments about detail and process.

---

13 National Audit Office (17th November 2006) *Delivering Successful IT-enabled Business Change*, Available at: http://www.nao.org.uk/publications/0607/delivering_successful_it-enabl.aspx [Last accessed: 13th December 2008].

The importance of leadership and governance is discussed further in Chapter 7.

Team Skills and the Project Portfolio Management Function

Whilst senior support helps ease the path, someone needs to address the detailed issues of implementing and operating the portfolio process day to day. The existence of a function able to drive the development of project portfolio management over an extended period and to provide the required analysis and reports to the governance bodies is therefore crucial. A popular choice is the establishment of a Portfolio Management Office – whether this is a formal or virtual structure will depend on the organisation (the size of its project portfolio, the existence of an existing Investment Management function and so on) although at least in the initial stages, experience indicates that it is important that sufficient concentrated effort can be devoted to establishing and operating the new processes.

Key roles for a Portfolio Management Office (either real or virtual) include:

- Designing, implementing and communicating the portfolio management processes – these should build on existing organisational processes where possible and encompass guidance on business case development, covering both the format in which proposals should be presented and the depth of analysis expected. This helps ensure a level playing field for investment appraisal and portfolio prioritisation. As we shall see in Chapter 4, business cases are not always based on reliable data. A key role for the Portfolio Management Office is therefore to design processes that incentivise reliable estimating (so building quality into the process rather than being based solely on detecting 'irrational exuberence') and incorporating robust independent appraisal that challenges the assumptions on which business cases and benefits realisation plans are based.

- Defining and agreeing, via the governance bodies, the investment criteria that will be used to appraise and prioritise potential investments.

- Appraising project proposals against the agreed investment criteria, undertaking analyses for stage gate and portfolio-level reviews, keeping project business cases under review and advising the governance bodies on resource allocation decisions.

- Advising project teams and business case writers on what is expected of them. Whilst the Portfolio Management Office needs to retain its independence so that it can appraise investments objectively, it should also work with projects and business units in improving investment submissions and progress reports.

- Producing clear and succinct portfolio performance reports on a regular basis encompassing project delivery status, expenditure against budget, benefits realisation against target, revised benefits forecast, portfolio-level risks and highlighting issues for management attention.

- Continually revising processes in the light of experience.

It is essential that the Portfolio Management Office has no responsibility for project and programme delivery – so that project appraisals are objective and are seen to be so. To independence and objectivity, we also need to add tenacity, in managing a process that brings discipline and scrutiny where perhaps there was little before, and credibility. The function therefore also needs access to relevant skills and competencies in organisational strategy, economics and financial analysis, as well as an understanding of project and programme management and delivery disciplines. Most importantly, it is crucial that the function does not adopt what we call a 'victim mentality' – too often we have seen cases where staff become discouraged and go through the motions because they believe they don't have a 100 per cent mandate to enforce the agreed process. All organisations are to some extent 'political' with decision making a combination of trade offs, management judgment and data driven analysis. The task of the Portfolio Management Office is to work within these constraints for the benefit of the enterprise as a whole and this requires a 'can do' attitude focused on the 'long game'. A sample role profile for a Portfolio Manager/Analyst is included as an Appendix to this chapter.

There is one other factor on which effective Project Portfolio Management relies and that's the adoption of a modular or incremental approach to projects. If Portfolio Management is to be an active process in which the collection of investments are managed in the light of performance, changed circumstances and organisational learning, then it is crucial that we are able to flex funding

---

EXAMPLE 6.   A PORTFOLIO MANAGEMENT FUNCTION

The CJS IT Portfolio Unit was established independent of any delivery function, to: undertake investment appraisals and portfolio prioritisation exercises; to ensure benefits were robust and realisable; to collate, analyse and report on portfolio progress; and to provide specialist advice to the governance bodies. The team was made up of a mix of permanent civil servants, contractors and consultants and had access to a range of skills – accountants, economists, business domain/ subject matter experts and benefits analysts. In this way it acted as an 'Intelligent Customer Function' providing analyses for the respective governance bodies.

---

allocations 'in flight'. If we are unable to redirect spend by adjusting resource allocation after the initial decision to invest, then our ability to manage our change projects and programmes as a portfolio will be severely constrained. It is therefore crucial that the organisation adopts a modular or incremental, rather than an 'all or nothing', approach to project planning and resource allocation. The McCartney Report[14] defined these approaches as follows:

- A module is *'a discrete part of an overall programme of work that offers some value to the organisation, even if the other parts of the programme are not completed'*.

- An incremental approach refers to where *'development begins with a component of the overall system that is deliberately limited in functionality, then builds on that component to increase its value to the organisation'*.

Once again senior management commitment is crucial – in encouraging project teams and business units to develop proposals that are truly modular or incremental, and in favouring such proposals over others in the resource allocation process. Besides facilitating active portfolio management, there's another advantage of this approach – it works! The McCartney report noted that research by Manchester University, Gartner and others, both in the UK and abroad, has found that large-scale change has a lower probability of success – breaking projects and programmes down into smaller chunks reduces risk, improves success rates and whilst there is some potential loss in total benefits, a modular approach provides greater certainty and earlier delivery of some benefits. The approach can be also be applied to implementation as well as to

---

14 Cabinet Office (2002) *Successful IT: Modernising Government in Action,* Available at: http:// archive.cabinetoffice.gov.uk/e-envoy/reports-itprojects/$file/successful_it.pdf [Last accessed: 15th November 2008].

development – for example, via pilots and phased implementation, which allows learning to be incorporated and the project to be adjusted to reflect changing requirements. The McCartney report proposed a guideline of a maximum timespan of 18 months from business case approval to project closure.

EXAMPLE 7. MODULAR PROJECTS AND PROGRAMMES – 'DOLPHINS NOT WHALES'

Mike Cross[1] reported in 2002 that the OECD had called on governments to avoid large IT projects and to create *'dolphins not whales'*. One example of this in practice is the 'Wiring Up Youth Justice' programme which started with the areas identified by the core business as their main areas of concern – making information available on *'who people are, where they are coming from and where they go after they've been with us'.*[2] A series of discrete projects were implemented that minimised dependencies, enabled technical solutions to be proved and early realisation of benefits. Sir Ian Magee commented in his report on improving Multi Agency Public Protection that, *'In Youth Justice, very modest investment has been used to make significant incremental improvements in getting critical information to move with the young offender across organizations at the right speed. In the present financial climate, the youth justice system could be useful across the Public Protection Network.'* From this basis the programme can potentially be extended to related services such as adult justice, case management and digital support for curfews and tagging. Mike Mackay, CIO, comments, *'Small pieces, loosely joined, nationally delivered, but locally steered. Using these approaches we've found a formula that lets us achieve grand end-to-end offender management and joining up goals, but not through traditional Hymalayan style, siege mentality programmes, but by small well understood, clearly designed increments. It works and the proof is there now. Can this approach be exploited elsewhere in government and at different scales: absolutely.'*

Another example of creating 'dolphins' rather than 'whales', comes from the cross-government 'Tell Us Once' programme – focusing initially on birth, death and bereavement, the programme can be extended in due course to other partners and services such as change of address once the solutions to cross-government information sharing are proven. Once again, the scale of investment is minimised, risks are controlled more effectively, and benefits are realised earlier.

---

1   Cross, M. (2002) 'Why Government IT Projects go Wrong', *Computing*, 12 September: pp. 37–40.
2   Veltech, M. (2009) 'New Peaks for Youth Justice', *CIO UK*, October, pp. 26–29.

Chapter 2 Conclusions and Take-aways

1.   A clearly articulated corporate strategy, top management support, a suitably skilled and independent portfolio analysis function and

modular or incremental project planning are the four prerequisites upon which effective repeatable project portfolio management processes can be built.

2. Expertise in project and programme management is clearly of value in improving delivery, but it reflects the means rather than the objectives of the change programme. Consequently Project and Programme Management skills contribute to portfolio success but they are not necessary prerequisites for a focus on aligning resource allocation with strategy. Similarly the use of software tools are not required for effective portfolio management. Organisations that seek a tool as their first step on the portfolio management road usually end up regretting it. Process and governance come first and the tool should be tailored to the process not vice versa. That said, appropriate use of software tools can help embed processes and this is covered further in Chapter 7. For the time being though, our attention now turns to the key portfolio management processes:

- in Chapter 3 we consider how to establish the portfolio regime – its scope and procedures;

- in Chapter 4 we examine Investment Management and how to prioritise and select investments at an individual and collective level;

- in Chapter 5 we then review how we can manage the portfolio 'in flight' on an active basis to ensure a balanced portfolio is maintained, with a high degree of strategic alignment and to optimise the return on investment in the light of changing circumstances, both organisational and environmental; and

- in Chapter 6 we bring it all together in considering benefits realisation and value management.

Appendix to Chapter 2: Role Profile – Portfolio Manager/Analyst

PURPOSE/OBJECTIVE

Developing and applying best practice portfolio management tools, techniques and repeatable processes to manage the [**insert name of organisation/business unit/function**] portfolio so ensuring that:

- funded projects meet, and continue to meet, minimum standards of attractiveness and achievability;

- the portfolio remains strategically aligned;

- the portfolio is balanced in terms of, attractiveness/achievability, project size, scale and complexity, and across the various strategic priorities; and

- the portfolio delivers the maximum impact in terms of realising financial benefits, contributing to strategic targets, and in managing the organisation's risk exposure.

MAIN ACTIVITIES

1. Managing periodic portfolio prioritisation reviews to determine funding priorities in the context of current business priorities encompassing:

    - Looking back – delivery against milestones; spend against budget; and benefits realised in terms of financial benefits (costs saved/revenue generated), impact on business priorities and reduction in risk exposure.

    - Looking forward – state of the project pipeline; capacity to absorb change; and forecast business impact in the next planning period.

    - Submitting the results of these reviews to the Portfolio Governance body including the preparation of relevant Portfolio Maps, with clear advice as to the conclusions reached.

2.   Undertaking Investment Appraisals – appraising business cases submitted by projects for funding including assessing:

- attractiveness – in terms of financial return and impact on strategic targets and business priorities; and

- achievability – in terms of technical achievability, project deliverability and the likelihood of benefits realisation.

Submitting the results of these reviews to the Portfolio Governance body with clear advice as to the conclusions reached.

3.   Compiling regular portfolio performance progress reports encompassing measures of: Delivery, Efficiency, Balance and Impact.

4.   Supporting the portfolio governance body by undertaking ad hoc reviews and producing reports and analyses as required.

5.   Maintaining the portfolio process and supporting guidelines and templates. Adapting these processes, guidelines and templates in response to issues identified by:

- project and programme post implementation reviews;

- regular independent reviews of the effectiveness of the portfolio process;

- environmental scanning to identify portfolio management best practice as used in other organisations; and

- submissions made under the 'Champion-Challenger' model (see Chapter 8).

6.   Advising project teams, business case writers and business change managers on the requirements of the portfolio process.

7.   Training staff in the Portfolio Management processes.

BEHAVIOURAL COMPETENCIES

The Portfolio Manager/Analyst needs a combination of: credibility (based on their professional skills); objectivity (derived from organisational independence from responsibility for project and programme delivery); and tenacity and commitment to adding value. This requires that the Portfolio Manager/Analyst work with business unit colleagues in the development of reliable business cases, project and programme staff in improving delivery, and business functions in realising benefits and creating value from the organisation's accumulated investment in change.

SKILLS FRAMEWORK FOR THE INFORMATION AGE (SFIA) COMPETENCIES (VERSION 3)[15]

#	Category, Sub-category, Skill	Level	Level description	Notes
1	Business change, Business change management, Programme management (PGMG) The identification, planning and coordination of a set of related projects within a programme of business change, to manage their interdependencies in support of specific business strategies. Maintains a strategic view over the set of projects, providing the framework for implementing business initiatives, or large-scale change, by achieving a vision of the outcome of the programme. The vision, and the means of achieving it, may change as the programme progresses.			
	Portfolio Analyst	6	Plans, directs and coordinates activities to manage and implement interrelated projects from contract/proposal initiation to final operational stage; plans, schedules, monitors and reports on activities related to the programme. Leads the programme teams in determining business requirements and translating requirements into operational plans. Determines, monitors and reviews all programme economics to include programme costs, operational budgets, staffing requirements, programme resources and programme risk. Ensures that the programme is managed to realise business benefits and that programme management is informed by an awareness of current technical developments.	Participates in investment appraisals and portfolio prioritisation exercises; drafts performance reports and delivery plans.

---

15 Information from the Skills Framework for the Information Age is reproduced by permission of the SFIA foundation.

#	Category, Sub-category, Skill	Level	Level description	Notes
	Portfolio Manager	7	Aligns the objectives for information systems activities with business change objectives and authorises the selection and planning of all related projects and activities. Plans, directs and coordinates activities to manage and implement complex inter-related projects from contract/proposal initiation to final operational stage. Plans, schedules, monitors and reports on activities related to the programme. Leads the programme teams in determining business requirements and translating requirements into operational plans. Determines, monitors and reviews all programme economics, including programme costs, operational budgets, staffing requirements, programme resources and programme risk, ensuring that there are appropriate and effective governance arrangements, supported by comprehensive reporting. Evaluates changes to programme management practices and initiates improvement to organisation practices.	Manages investment appraisals and portfolio prioritisation exercises; presents performance reports to the portfolio governance body.
2	Strategy and planning, Information strategy, Information management (IRMG) The overall management of information, as a fundamental business resource, to ensure that the information needs of the business are met. Encompasses development and promotion of the strategy and policies covering the design of information structures and taxonomies, the setting of policies for the sourcing and maintenance of the data content, the management and storage of electronic content and the analysis of information structure (including logical analysis of data and metadata). Includes overall responsibility for compliance with regulations, standards and codes of good practice relating to information and documentation records management, information assurance and data protection.			
	Portfolio Analyst	5	Takes responsibility for planning effective electronic information storage, sharing and publishing within the organisation. Maintains and communicates the organisation's information management strategy. Devises and implements electronic document and record systems, including classification, retrieval and retention processes. Maintains an inventory of information subject to data protection legislation. Reviews new business proposals and provides specialist advice on information management, including advice on and promotion of collaborative working. Responsible for ensuring compliance with organisational policies and procedures and overall information management strategy.	Responsible for collecting, analysing and reporting portfolio-level information on progress against: targets, milestones, budget, risks and benefits.

#	Category, Sub-category, Skill	Level	Level description	Notes
	Portfolio Manager	6	Maintains and communicates the organisation's strategy for managing information, ensuring that uniformly recognised and accepted data definitions are developed and applied throughout the organisation. Models the processes and information required to support the organisation and devises corresponding data structures and architectures. Identifies the impact of any relevant statutory, internal or external regulations on the organisation's use of information.	Develops and agrees the Portfolio Management regime with the portfolio governance body; manages the production of periodic performance reports for the governance body utilising the 'one version of the truth' principle.
3	Strategy and planning, Advice and guidance, Consultancy (CNSL) The provision of advice, assistance and leadership in any area associated with the planning, procurement, provision, delivery, management, maintenance or effective use of information systems and their environments. The consultancy can deal with one specific aspect of IT and the business, or it can be wide ranging and address strategic business issues.			
	Portfolio Analyst	5	Provides well-informed advice, typically within a specific technical specialism, ensuring that it is properly understood and appropriately exploited, to enhance the effectiveness of significant activities.	Provides advice and guidance to business case writers and project staff on the requirements for funding including: the investment criteria; evidence required; completing standard template submissions; the investment appraisal process (inc. timescales) and process for reporting results to the governance body.
	Portfolio Manager	6	Manages provision of specialist knowledge over a range of topics including the role of IT in the business; in own areas of expertise provides advice and guidance influencing the effectiveness of the organisation's business processes.	Provides advice and guidance to business managers on the portfolio management processes and requirements for funding.
4	Strategy and planning, Advice and guidance, Technical specialism (TECH) The management and provision of expert advice on a specific technical specialism. Examples of specialism can be any technology, technique, method, product or application area.			
	Portfolio Analyst	5	Maintains knowledge of specific technical specialisms, provides detailed advice regarding their application, executes specialised tasks. The specialism can be any area of information or communication technology, technique, method, product or application area.	Maintains professional knowledge of investment appraisal and portfolio prioritisation techniques; maintains an up-to-date understanding of the business priorities which the portfolio is designed to deliver.

#	Category, Sub-category, Skill	Level	Level description	Notes
	Portfolio Manager	6	Maintains an in-depth knowledge of specific technical specialisms and provides expert advice regarding their application. Can supervise specialist technical consultancy. The specialism can be any aspect of information or communication technology, technique, method, product or application area.	Maintains professional knowledge of investment appraisal and portfolio prioritisation techniques; maintains an up-to-date understanding of the business priorities which the portfolio is designed to deliver.
5	Strategy and planning, Business/information systems strategy and planning, Business risk management (BURM) The planning and implementation of organisation-wide processes and procedures for the management of operational risk.			
	Portfolio Manager	5	Carries out risk assessment within a defined functional or technical area of business. Uses consistent processes for identifying potential risk events, quantifying and documenting the probability of occurrence and impact on the business. Refers to domain experts for guidance on specialised areas of risk, such as architecture and environment. Coordinates the development of countermeasures and contingency plans.	Assesses portfolio-level risk as part of the periodic portfolio-level reviews; maintains the portfolio-level Risk Register; and advises the governance body on the overall level of portfolio risk.
6	Business Change, Relationship management, Stakeholder relationship management (RLMT) The coordination of relationships with and between key stakeholders, during the design, management and implementation of business change.			
	Portfolio Analyst	5	Develops and manages one or more defined communication channels and/or stakeholder groups. Initiates communications between stakeholders, acting as a single point of contact for defined groups. Facilitates open communication and discussion between stakeholders. Captures and disseminates technical and business information. Facilitates the business change decision-making processes and the planning and implementation of change.	Ensures the portfolio management process is understood by all relevant parties. Provides a programme of ongoing training for project, business and portfolio staff.

#	Category, Sub-category, Skill	Level	Level description	Notes
	Portfolio Manager	6	Initiates and influences relationships with and between key stakeholders. Acts as a single point of contact for senior stakeholders and influencers. Supports effective business change by building relationships with and between senior strategists, planners, designers and operational business partners. Initiates procedures to improve relations and open communications with and between stakeholders. Initiates and has management oversight of processes to manage and monitor relationships including lessons learned and the feedback loop to and from business change teams.	Liaises with and maintains effective working relationships with: project teams, business case writers and business change managers.

3

Key Process 1: Establishing the Portfolio

'Well begun is half done.'

Aristotle

After reading this chapter you will:

- have an understanding of the four elements in establishing the portfolio – deciding on the scope of the portfolio; agreeing standardised processes and guidelines; determining the investment criteria to be used to select and prioritise potential investments; and segmenting the portfolio;
- realise that rather than representing an additional bureaucracy, correctly applied, portfolio management can streamline existing processes and so deliver efficiency savings.

Introduction

This stage lays the basis for all that follows – deciding where to invest, managing the project portfolio 'in flight' and realising the benefits. But this does not mean that we apply these processes sequentially, rather we refine and adapt each process as we progress. Establishing the portfolio encompasses four elements:

1. Deciding on the scope of the portfolio – which projects, programmes and other initiatives are included in the portfolio and which are excluded.

2. Agreeing standardised processes, templates and guidance.

3. Determining the investment criteria to guide investment decisions.

4.   Portfolio segmentation – splitting the portfolio into organisationally appropriate categories for example, by project type and/or investment objective – and then tailoring the investment criteria to the various portfolio segments.

These are considered in turn.

1. Deciding on the Scope of the Portfolio

This requires agreement on a common definition of what constitutes a project or programme (as opposed to 'business as usual') and which types of projects (information technology, organisational change, construction, acquisition and so on) are to be included in the portfolio. The most common approach is to set a minimum threshold level below which initiatives are excluded from the portfolio, but these limits need to be set with care – too low and the Investment Board risks being overwhelmed, and too high can mean that much of the change agenda won't appear on the change portfolio 'radar'. At the same time there need to be effective checks in place to prevent projects being disaggregated deliberately so that they come in under the threshold level and so avoid portfolio governance. One solution is to set the threshold at a level that ensures the governance bodies review only the major investments but with two caveats – firstly that all projects with a cross-organisational or major operational impact are included, and secondly, to review the entire spend on a periodic basis.

2. Standardisation of Process, Templates and Guidance

Cooper, Edgett and Kleinschmidt (1999)[1] report that '*the great majority of the top businesses (77.5 percent) use a formal portfolio management system*'. Formal does not however mean bureaucratic – the objective here is to streamline processes to ensure that everyone is clear about how much analysis is required and what standards of documentation and evidence are required and when – with more detail being required as the financial commitments increase. This includes guidelines on measuring and valuing costs and benefits that apply to all business cases to minimise double counting and facilitate a consistent approach across the portfolio, that is, a level playing field which enables comparisons over time

---

1   Cooper, R. G., Edgett, S. J. and Kleinschmidt, E. J. (1998) 'Best Practices for Managing R&D Portfolios', *Research Technology Management*, July-August, pp. 20–33. Re-printed in Dye, L. D. and Pennypacker, J. S. (eds) (1999) *Project Portfolio Management*, Glen Mills, PA.

and between projects. This can also realise efficiency savings as all projects work to common processes and standards.

These processes should cover the investment life cycle from project proposal and entry to the portfolio, preparing business cases, investment appraisal and portfolio prioritisation, releasing funds, and tracking performance through to project closure and evaluation. Implementation needs to be supported by an ongoing training programme to communicate the processes across the organisation.

Contrary to common practice, a good business case is not a long business case. Indeed experience suggests that there is often an inverse relationship between the length of a business case and its quality! Let's be clear – I'm not suggesting that detailed analysis of requirements, options appraisal and benefits should not occur, only that presenting a 200-page document is no guarantee of *quality* analysis. Indeed, a 'good' business case writer can hide an enormous amount of information in 100 pages, and even more in 150 pages. Size in this context is the enemy of understanding – so take the opportunity to:

- Define a simple and succinct summary business case template so that there is a shared understanding of the investment and its:

    - *Attractiveness* – the investment justification in terms of financial return, strategic impact or meeting a mandatory requirement. The reader should be clear as to why the investment is being undertaken and what benefits you are buying – for example:

        o Cashable savings – how much will be saved in budgetary or unit cost terms and when?

        o Non-cashable efficiency savings – how much time will be saved and what exactly will this saving be used for, with what impact, and when (noting that staff time savings are effectively a voucher or potential benefit where the value depends on what the time saved is used for)?

        o Strategic impacts – what scale of contribution to strategic priorities will be achieved, when, and how will this be measured?

–   *Achievability* – in terms of technical and project deliverability as well as benefits realisation; and

–   *Affordability* – both upfront investment and ongoing running costs.

EXAMPLE 8.   SUMMARY REPORTING

The CJS IT Programme introduced a three-page 'Triple A' investment appraisal report – with one page each for:

- Attractiveness – the Net Present Value (NPV), Internal Rate of Return (IRR), payback period, scale of strategic contribution (using the OGC approach shown in Example 11), and benefits summary – by type and recipient (and whether anyone had signed up to realising the benefits claimed).
- Achievability – using the framework outlined in Chapter 4 – assessing degree of complexity, quality of planning and capacity to drive progress.
- Affordability – required capital and operating costs for the planning period and assumed sources of funds (including any recycling of benefits to pay for the project).

This provided the portfolio governance bodies with a succinct and consistent summary of the merits of all potential investments.

- Shift the emphasis from using business cases as a way of getting funding to a value-based document used throughout the project life cycle from selection, through control to evaluation. The focus should shift from the usual practice of trying to find sufficient benefits to justify the cost of the investment, to asking is it worth spending £x to realise the forecast benefits?

3. Investment Criteria

Detailed rules should be developed for particular classes of investment (more on this below and in the next chapter), but objective high-level investment criteria should be agreed to guide investment and reinvestment decisions so that everyone is clear about the criteria that are used to appraise competing investments.

EXAMPLE 9.   THE CJS IT INVESTMENT CRITERIA

The nine Investment Principles developed to guide investments in the CJS IT portfolio were as follows:

1.   All projects funded by the CJS IT ring-fence budget are subject to HM Treasury's Settlement Conditions and CJS IT governance arrangements.
2.   Projects must contribute to the CJS Vision and/or add value to multiple organisations.
3.   What has been started should be finished – funding should continue for those projects that are on time and to budget, otherwise previous investment would be wasted.[1]
4.   No new projects should be funded unless they can demonstrate a positive NPV with benefits agreed in principle by all parties.
5.   Options selected should represent: shortest implementation time, lowest cost and deliver a reasonable amount of benefit.
6.   Overspends should be borne by the relevant organisation rather than the ring-fence budget.
7.   Continued funding will be contingent on project performance and will be reviewed periodically.
8.   Projects will not be funded if critical issues are unresolved.
9.   Projects should meet best-practice thresholds for Attractiveness and Achievability.

Developing such criteria doesn't need to take long – the above criteria were developed in a half-hour planning session and were found to stand the test of time.

---

1   Readers will note that this was in effect an implicit admittance that some of the projects within this particular portfolio were not really modular in nature. This was the reality in relation to several large projects that were already well advanced when the portfolio was established. This also illustrates the point explored in Chapter 7 that moving to a fully effective portfolio approach can take several years.

---

4. Portfolio Segmentation

One approach to portfolio prioritisation is to appraise all potential investments against the agreed investment criteria and then work down the list from the highest ranking project until available funds (or another limiting factor) are exhausted. The primary problem with this approach of comparing all projects against the same set of criteria is that it can result in an unbalanced portfolio as long-term capacity building projects are excluded in favour of, for example, projects with a quick financial payback – but long-term performance may suffer without sufficient investment in capability and capacity enhancing projects.

Similarly, depending on the investment criteria used, we can end up with a disproportionate investment in higher return/risk projects as opposed to lower return, but more achievable projects. Related to this is the concern that using one investment criterion can encourage game playing as projects tailor their cases to the criteria set rather than the real investment objective.

An approach that can help overcome these issues is to segment the portfolio by splitting available funds into organisationally appropriate categories, and then prioritise investments in each segment using criteria appropriate to that category. Once complete, there is a final check that the overall portfolio is balanced and represents the optimum use of investment funds to the organisation as a whole. One such segmentation approach is that proposed by Ward and Peppard (2002) (see Figure 3.1).[2] Whilst Ward and Peppard were concerned with IS/IT projects, the framework proposed is equally applicable to other types of investment.

Strategic	**High Potential**
Investments in IS/IT applications which are critical to sustaining future business strategy	Investments in IS/IT applications which may be important in achieving future success
Key Operational	**Support**
Investments in IS/IT applications on which the organisation currently depends for success	Investments in IS/IT applications which are valuable but not critical to success

Figure 3.1   The Cranfield Information Systems Investment Portfolio

Another approach from the IT field comes from Peter Weill, Director of the Center for Information Systems Research at the Sloan School of Management, Massachusetts Institute of Technology (MIT). He argues that IT investment should be managed as a portfolio with four asset classes, each with their own investment objectives. As with financial portfolio management, the IT portfolio needs to be balanced across the four asset classes (or segments) to ensure alignment with business strategy in both the short and long term (see Figure 3.2).

Analysis of IT spend in this manner facilitates consideration as to whether resources are appropriately distributed in the context of environmental conditions and business priorities. The value of such analyses is that they

---

2   Ward, J. M. and Peppard, J. (2002) *Strategic Planning for Information Systems,* 3rd ed, John Wiley & Sons, Chichester.

Asset Class	Description	Investment Objective[a]
Strategic	Applications to support entry into a new market, development of new or customised products etc.	To gain competitive advantage or position in the market place.
Informational	Applications providing information to manage, account, control, plan, comply, report and communicate with customers.	To provide more and better information for any purpose including to account, manage, control, report, communicate, collaborate or analyse.
Transactional	Applications to automate repetitive transactions, cut costs and increase throughput.	To cut costs or increase throughput so reducing unit costs and increasing productivity.
Infrastructure	Shared IT services such as the network, customer databases, pc/laptops, help desks, data centres, servers, security, middleware but not applications.	Base foundation of shared IT services used by multiple applications. Such investments can be to reduce cost via standardisation or consolidation and/or to provide a flexible platform for future business initiatives.

[a]   Weill, P. and Aral, S. (2004) 'Managing the IT Portfolio: Returns From The Different IT Asset Classes', MIT Sloan Center for Information Systems Research, Research Briefing, IV: 1A, March 2004.

Figure 3.2   The MIT four asset classes

EXAMPLE 10.   SEGMENTATION IN THE CJS IT PORTFOLIO

The portfolio was segmented with investment criteria being tailored to the type of project as shown below.

Business applications

Justified on cost-benefit terms i.e. does the economic value exceed the costs (in present value terms)?

Politically mandated projects and legal/regulatory requirements

Justified on cost-benefit terms with any shortfall representing the 'political value' on a willingness to pay basis of avoiding non-compliance with law, regulation or policy.

Replacement infrastructure

Justified on cost-effectiveness terms i.e. does the replacement enable resources to be redirected to other value-adding activities?

> **New infrastructure**
>
> Justified on cost-benefit terms by taking into consideration both the infrastructure and the applications (planned and potential) that will run on that infrastructure.

enable comparisons against plan, other organisations, and over time, as well as being used to target reductions in infrastructure spend, so releasing resources for business value-adding applications. Another framework as used on the CJS IT portfolio is outlined in Example 10 on page 45.

The above approaches are variations on the theme of segmentation by project type – each has merit and can indeed be used in combination, but a recommended approach is to segment the portfolio according to the primary investment objective or strategic driver, and then to tailor the investment criteria to those investment objectives. Projects will generally fall into one of the following categories based on their strategic driver or investment objective, and the relevant investment criteria then reflect the purpose for which the investment is being made:

- *Revenue generation* – where selection and prioritisation should be on the basis of greatest financial 'bang' for your 'buck' most usually measured by NPV (or more correctly, NPV per unit of limiting factor where a constraint exists – the so-called 'Productivity Index' – more on this below).

- *Cost savings/efficiency* – where again, selection and prioritisation should be on the basis of NPV.

- *Strategic contribution* – potential investments in this segment should be prioritised on the basis of strategic contribution per £ invested. This is clearly more problematic to quantify although approaches to addressing this issue are outlined in the next chapter. This segment can also be sub-divided into sub-segments for each main strategy.

- *'Must do' projects* – those that are a legal or regulatory requirement or are required to maintain business as usual. The usual investment criteria will be lowest net present cost, that is, meeting the requirement at lowest cost. Be careful though – projects can claim to be mandatory to avoid portfolio governance. The key is to ensure the source of any mandate (legal or regulatory requirement) is clear along with the implications of non-compliance. This should be supported by two additional pieces of analysis: firstly, one showing how the project will meet the mandate, and secondly, one showing that this could not be achieved by another means more cost-effectively.

Ultimately more than one view can be taken to ensure the portfolio remains aligned with strategy and is balanced – although the approach outlined above is recommended as it directly relates the investment criteria to the investment objectives and supports a value management approach. Segmentation also helps ensure the portfolio is strategically aligned by ensuring high-level funding allocation reflects strategic priorities. Approaches to determining whether individual initiatives are strategically aligned are covered in the next chapter.

Chapter 3 Conclusions and Take-aways

Establishing the change portfolio encompasses four elements:

1. Deciding on the scope of the portfolio – which projects, programmes and other change initiatives will be included and which are excluded. Beware overload, and watch out for disaggregation of proposals to avoid portfolio governance. A Portfolio Management Office can play a valuable role here in balancing these pressures and ensuring a clear line of sight across the whole change portfolio.

2. Agreeing standardised processes, templates and guidance – take the opportunity to streamline documentation to focus on the key data and shift the focus from costs to value. Business cases should *'start with the end in mind'*.

3. Determining the investment criteria that will be used to select and prioritise investments.

4. Portfolio segmentation – splitting the portfolio into organisationally appropriate categories for example, by project type and/or investment objective – and then tailoring the investment criteria to the various portfolio segments.

4

Key Process 2: Investment Management

'A task always takes longer than you expect, even when you take into account Hofstadter's Law.'

Douglas Hofstadter

After reading this chapter you will:

- understand the need to consider a project's attractiveness in the context of its achievability;
- know how to assess a project's 'attractiveness' and 'achievability';
- understand the issues associated with the reliability of the estimates of costs and benefits commonly used in business cases – and the issues of 'optimism bias' and 'strategic misrepresentation'. Solutions to these issues are also covered;
- recognise the importance of considering the attractiveness and achievability of investments from a collective portfolio-level perspective and the key factors to consider in making this assessment.

Introduction

The objective in allocating investment funds is to maximise the return, however this is defined, over the long term. The lessons from portfolio management in the financial securities field are that firstly, we need to consider individual returns in the context of risk, that is, an investment might have a fantastic return but how risky is it? As Ward (2006) says, *'The more successful organisations select projects on the basis of desirability and their capability to deliver them, not just desirability.'*[1] So consideration of risk and return in financial security portfolio

---

1 Ward, J. (August 2006) *Delivering Value from Information Systems and Technology Investments: Learning from success*, A report of the results of an international survey of Benefits Management Practices in 2006.

management is matched in project portfolio management by consideration of value, desirability or attractiveness (including both financial and non-financial benefits) in the context of viability, deliverability or achievability (including technical and project deliverability as well as confidence in benefits realisation).

Secondly, we need to consider the portfolio of projects and programmes as a whole, that is, taking into account dependencies, inter-dependencies and constraints, is it balanced overall in terms of strategic coverage, in terms of short and longer-term return and are risks at a collective level acceptable?

We consider investment appraisal at the individual project level before turning to the issue of portfolio-level prioritisation. But first one stake in the ground – I advocate treating projects, programmes and other change initiatives as INVESTMENTS – this terminology focuses attention on the fact that success does not equate to delivery of the project but to the realisation of the benefits from that investment. We will examine value and benefits management further in Chapter 6, but it is important to realise that effective value management starts with, and even before, the preparation of the business case. So let's talk investments.

Project Selection and Investment Appraisal

How do we appraise potential projects and prioritise them for investment, that is, how do we sift the 'good' from the 'bad', the 'attractive' from the 'ugly' and how do we maximise the 'bang' from our 'buck'? The answer it would appear is far from straightforward – research by Lambert and Edwards (2003)[2] found that most organisations felt their investment appraisal processes were ineffective with 78 per cent responding 'no' to the question, '*Do you have an effective investment appraisal process?*' Addressing this calls for consideration of both the techniques that we use to appraise investments and the organisational dynamics that influence how these appraisals are used, and the reliability of the data on which they are based. We first consider the techniques used – most approaches fall into one of two categories: financial techniques and management scorecards incorporating Multi-Criteria Analysis (MCA). We then consider the

---

2   Lambert, R. and Edwards, C. (2003) *A Survey of IS/IT Project Appraisal*, IS Group, Cranfield School of Management. Quoted in Ward, J. and Daniel, E. (2006) *Benefits Management Delivering Value from IS & IT Investments*, John Wiley & Sons, Chichester.

issue of data reliability and how we can best utilise this data to inform our investment decisions.

FINANCIAL APPRAISAL TECHNIQUES

Traditionally the most popular investment appraisal methods were payback (how long will it take before the total cash inflows repay the total cash outflows?) and accounting rate of return (profit generated divided by the cost of the investment). These techniques suffer from one overriding deficiency however, in that they take no account of the time value of money, that is, a pound today is worth more than a pound in a year's time – for example, with inflation of 5 per cent, £100 will only be worth £78 in five years time. Consequently modern management accounting recommends the use of discounting techniques in the form of IRR and NPV. Under these approaches the future incremental cash flows are discounted at the organisation's cost of capital (3.5 per cent in central government as specified by the HM Treasury Green Book) to calculate the IRR and/or the NPV, that is, the project's future cash flows expressed at today's value. Past investments are regarded as 'sunk' and are consequently excluded from the calculation – in other words, the decision to invest or continue to invest should be based on future cash flows only. This is however premised on those cash flows being accurate, and as we shall see, this is often not the case in relation to both costs and benefits.

There are reasons for not ignoring sunk costs entirely, not least because they can be an important indicator of project health – if a project can only show a positive return by continually shifting the 'starting line', that is a red flag about the original forecasts contained in the business case and potentially, the project's achievability. Thus, at the least, continued transparency on the full life cost-benefit position promotes accountability and forces questions as to why the cost-benefit position has deteriorated and, looking forward, what action has been taken to contain this? Keeping an eye on the total life cost-benefit position and being aware of the total investment required can also act as a stimulus to identifying additional benefits to cover any cost escalation. I also recommend that key project metrics should include not only the NPV, but also the time taken to recover the investment (the payback) and the depth of the investment, that is, how far do we go into 'the red' before benefits start to exceed the incremental costs? These are useful indicators of project risk.

Putting such considerations of sunk costs aside, the theoretically 'correct' approach is to rank projects according to their NPV, although where there is a constraint, the NPV should be divided by the unit of the constraining or limiting factor – this is the so-called 'Productivity Index' and shows how much money at today's value will be delivered from a unit of the limiting factor such as funding, availability of skilled resources or indeed, the business change capacity of the organisation.[3] We will not review the technicalities of these methods further as computer spreadsheets mean that anyone with basic training can run the NPV and IRR calculations and readers with a desire to investigate further are referred to any standard management accountancy textbook[4] that will address them in detail (including the technical issues with IRR and why NPV is usually the technique of choice[5]). What should be noted, however, is that the HM Treasury Green Book recommends the use of cost-benefit analysis, whereby monetary values are attributed, wherever feasible, to all costs and benefits including those where there is no market value.[6] NPV (using a real[7] discount factor of 3.5 per cent reflecting social time preference) is the preferred decision criterion, that is, projects are expected to show a positive NPV when the economic value of the benefits is compared with the project costs.

There are, however, three main problems with the financial approaches to project and programme appraisal and prioritisation, including cost-benefit analysis. Firstly, they are premised on estimates of future cash flows being reliable. Unfortunately evidence would indicate that this is often not the case. Beyond the difficulties in determining monetary value where there are no market prices (the value of a life saved or the reduction in risk of environmental damage for example) both costs and benefits are likely to vary from initial forecast because we are dealing with an uncertain future. There are, however, other factors at play that have less to do with future uncertainty and more to do with the way in which we develop forecasts and the context in which they are made – this is discussed further below under the heading 'Data Reliability'.

---

3   Where there is more than one limiting factor or constraint, mathematical modelling approaches are available in many of the leading portfolio management software packages. The calculations are however subject to the point made elsewhere about the risks of pursuing a spurious degree of accuracy.

4   For example, *Management and Cost Accounting* by Drury (2000) Business Press, or *Principles of Corporate Finance* (1991) by Brealey and Myers published by McGraw Hill.

5   Indeed, the HMT Green Book advises that IRR should be avoided because it can in some circumstances lead to '*incorrect, answers*'.

6   In such circumstances techniques such as stated and revealed preference can be used to determine value on a 'willingness to pay' basis. For further information see HM Treasury (2003) *The Green Book Appraisal and Evaluation in Central Government*, TSO, London.

7   In other words, costs and benefits expressed at today's valuation with no adjustment for general inflation.

So what's the scale of this 'prediction error'? Examples of cost overruns such as the Sydney Opera House (1400 per cent), Concorde (1100 per cent) and the Channel Tunnel (80 per cent for construction and 140 per cent for financing costs)[8] grab the headlines, but are they representative of a more general trend? Mott MacDonald undertook a study for HM Treasury in 2002[9] of 50 large public procurement projects costing over £40m at 2001 prices. The sample covered a 20-year period and they found that average levels of cost underestimation at Outline Business Case stage in traditional procurement projects were in the order of: works duration 17 per cent; capital expenditure 47 per cent; and operating expenditure 41 per cent. Optimism bias was also found to affect benefits forecasts but reliable estimates of the scale of overestimation were not possible because in many cases the benefits had not been estimated in the first place or no attempt had been made to measure the scale of benefits realised. Mott MacDonald concluded that *'historically there has been a tendency for project estimates to be highly optimistic'*.

Other studies have come to similar conclusions. Flyvbjerg et al. (2002)[10] for example, undertook a four-year study of 258 transport infrastructure projects of various types (road, rail and fixed link, for example, bridges and tunnels) in 20 countries worldwide between 1927 and 1998, worth $90bn at 1995 prices. They concluded, *'It is found with overwhelming statistical significance that the cost estimates used to decide whether such projects should be built are highly and systematically misleading.'* This pattern held for projects irrespective of region, type or historical period – and unlike the Mott McDonald study, they found no evidence that things are getting better. Just in case it was felt that transportation projects might be regarded as somehow peculiar, they also reviewed the data for several hundred other types of project including IT, power plants, oil and gas extraction, weapons and aerospace. The conclusions were no less damning: *'The data indicate that other types of infrastructure project are at least as, if not more, prone to cost underestimation as are transportation infrastructure projects.'* A separate study by the same researchers of demand forecasting[11] in road and rail projects found that *'forecasters generally do a poor job of estimating the demand for transport infrastructure projects'*. The average overestimation in rail projects was 106 per

---

8   wikipedia.rog/wiki/cost_overrun.
9   MacDonald, M. (2002) Review of Large Public Procurement in the UK, Available at: http://www.hm-treasury.gov.uk/d/7(3).pdf [Last accessed: 1st December 2008].
10 Flyvbjerg, B., Mette, K., Skamris, H. and Søren, L. B. (2002) 'Underestimating Costs in Public Works Projects: Error or Lie?', *Journal of the American Planning Association*, 68:3, pp. 279–295.
11 Flyvbjerg, B., Mette, K., Skamris, H. and Søren, L. B. (2005) 'How (In)accurate Are Demand Forecasts in Public Works Projects', *Journal of the American Planning Association*, 71:2, Spring 2005.

cent but even with road projects around half had more than +/- 20 per cent estimation error (measured against estimates at Full Business Case stage). As with costs, they found that forecasts had not become more accurate over the 30 years covered by the study. The causes of this are discussed below under the heading 'Data Reliability' but for the time being it is sufficient to note that these findings (and in particular the combination of cost underestimation and benefit overestimation) severely compromise the reliability of the data used to make investment selection and portfolio prioritisation decisions.

This risk of variability in return (due to project achievability, cost escalation and benefits realisation shortfalls) can be accommodated in a number of ways:

1. Increasing the discount rate to reflect project risk – for example, by using one rate for low-risk projects, another for medium-risk projects and the highest rate for high-risk projects.

2. Rather than using single point estimates, probabilities can be assigned to a range of outcomes and the expected value can be calculated using Monte Carlo simulation[12] or more simply, using the PERT formula: [Optimistic Outcome + Pessimistic Outcome + 4 × the Most Likely Outcome] divided by six. Linked to this, we should expect to see the degree of confidence in forecasts increase as we progress through development and this should be reflected in a narrowing of the range of forecasts presented.

3. Sensitivity analysis can be used to determine how the investment case is affected by changes in key factors and 'switching values' can be calculated to show by how much key factors have to change to alter the investment decision.

4. The HM Treasury Green Book requires business case estimates to be adjusted by increasing costs and delaying the realisation of benefits. The Green Book states that these adjustments for optimism bias should be empirically based, that is, they should be based on data derived from past, similar projects, although where such data is not available, the generic guidance can be used – for example, for equipment projects and those concerned with the development

---

12 For example, see the HMT Green Book Annex 4.

of software and systems, the supplementary guidance[13] quotes optimism bias adjustments of:

- Works duration – upper bound value 54 per cent, lower bound value 10 per cent;

- Capital expenditure – upper bound value 200 per cent, lower bound value 10 per cent.

The upper limit represents the average level of optimism bias found at Outline Business Case stage[14] by the Mott MacDonald study. This can be reduced by effective mitigation of the 21 factors identified by the study as contributing to optimism bias – these factors are grouped into five categories: procurement related; project specific; client specific; environmental; and external. The lower level of optimism bias represents the level that should be reached by the time the contract is awarded.

The approaches outlined above have merit in that they attempt to adjust for the risk of variability in return and project achievability. There is however no 'silver bullet' solution:

- adjusting the discount rate leads to the immediate question, *'by how much?'*;

- probability-based approaches are dependent upon accurate estimates of probabilities and yet research (see for example, Kahneman and Tversky, Taleb and Ayers[15]) has found that even experts can be remarkably poor in estimating probabilities. The other point to note about expected value approaches (where the various possible outcomes are assigned probabilities and the expected value is then the sum of these outcomes multiplied by

13 Supplementary Green Book Guidance, Available at: http://www.hm-treasury.gov.uk/data_ greenbook_supguidance.htm, [Last accessed: 13th December 2008].

14 Although the report from Mott MacDonald notes that the *'exceptionally high capital expenditure optimism bias for traditionally procured equipment and development projects was greatly affected by a single project.'* Whether the quoted rate is empirically sound is therefore open to some debate and emphasises the importance of organisations monitoring their own performance in project delivery, cost containment and benefits realisation.

15 Kahneman, D. and Tversky, A. (1979) 'Prospect Theory: An Analysis of Decisions under Risk', *Econometrica*, 47:2, pp 263–291. Cited in Flyvbjerg et al. (2002); Taleb, N. N. (2004) *Fooled by Randomness*, Penguin, London; Ayres, I. (2007) *Supercrunchers, Why Thinking-By-Numbers Is the New Way To Be Smart*, Bantam, New York.

their probabilities) is that the result is the average value that would be expected if the project was repeated a large number of times – an assumption that rarely holds true in practice; and

• adjusting cash flows for optimism bias based on past project performance may not be appropriate if we don't have reliable data on past performance[16] or if future conditions are likely to be different from the past. There is also the risk that forecasters will become even more optimistic in their estimating to take account of the fact that adjustments to their estimates will be made.

Such issues are put into context by the conclusions of Collins and Bicknell (1997)[17] that large ICT project disasters might have been avoided if '…*the costs of the new systems had been calculated meticulously and then multiplied by three'*. Even more worrying, a recent article by Paul Jackson[18] concludes that the advice appears to still hold true!

The second problem with financially-based investment appraisal techniques concerns their suitability when the investment objective is to support an organisational strategy, provide infrastructure, meet a mandatory requirement or organisational necessity such as maintaining current operations, that is, any situation where there is no obvious market value for the benefits or no immediate financial impact such as costs saved or revenue generated. The issue is that such projects may well not have a positive NPV, at least in the short term, and requiring them to demonstrate a positive return encourages business case writers to assign what are often arbitrary monetary values to non-financial benefits. There are methods for valuing such benefits, but assigning monetary values to non-monetary benefits can confuse the true nature of the investment case. The rule is as always, be clear about what benefits you are buying. In many instances you are not buying a financial return so let's not pretend that you are – indeed representing such investments as having a positive financial return on investment can be dangerous as it confuses a financial return with benefits that have an attributed economic value. This can divert attention from actually managing these investments so that benefits are realised and value is

---

16 Note for example that the Mott MacDonald study was of a relatively small sample of projects (50), over an extended time period (20 years) and no sound conclusions could be reached in relation to operating cost and benefits optimism bias levels due to lack of available data.

17 Collins, T. with Bicknell, D. (1997) *Crash Learning from the World's Worst Computer Disasters*, Simon and Schuster, London.

18 Jackson, P. (2009) 'Keeping it Simple: Avoiding the Dangers of Big IT Projects', *CIPFA Pinpoint*, Issue 8, March, pp. 6–8.

created. The approach I recommend is therefore that yes, cost-benefit appraisal should be undertaken where possible to determine that the economic value of the benefits exceeds the costs required – but in addition, I strongly believe that this should be enhanced by a financial NPV calculation which shows the net present cost required to realise the forecast non-financial benefits. Management can then come to an informed decision as to whether it's worth spending £x to get the defined operational or strategic benefits.

Thirdly, research has shown that these problems with financial appraisal techniques can have real world impacts – for example, Lin et al. (2005)[19] refer to problems with using traditional financial investment appraisal metrics in the cost-benefit appraisal of IS/IT investments and research by Cooper et al. (2001)[20] has found that *'an over-reliance on strictly financial data and criteria may lead to wrong portfolio decisions, simply because the financial data are often wrong!'* and *'they yielded the poorest results on just about every portfolio performance metric'*. The problem is that where costs and benefits are uncertain, financially-based investment appraisal techniques can encourage a degree of confidence that is not justified by the data used in the calculations. This, along with the problems in using financial measures to appraise investments that have non-financial objectives, has contributed to an increased interest in alternative approaches based on the use of management scorecards utilising MCA and combining consideration of investment attractiveness with that of project achievability.

MANAGEMENT SCORECARDS AND MULTI-CRITERIA ANALYSIS (MCA)[21]

Under this approach a series of factors judged to be relevant to investment decision making and portfolio prioritisation are identified and weighted. Potential investments are then scored to produce a ranked list of projects – either all projects or one for each segment. The HM Treasury Green Book suggests that such weighting and scoring methods can be used to assess unvalued costs and benefits, although the approach can be extended to incorporate both quantitative and qualitative factors. The advantages of this approach include the ability to tailor criteria and weightings to the particular organisational circumstances. Additionally, the

---

19 Lin, C., Pervan, G. and McDermid, D. (2005) 'IS/IT Investment Evaluation and Benefits Realization Issues in Australia', *Journal of Research and Practice in Information Technology*, 37:3, pp. 235–251.

20 Cooper, R. G., Edgett, S. J. and Kleinschmidt, E. J. (2001) *Portfolio Management for New Products*, 2nd ed, Perseus Press, Cambridge Mass.

21 A good overview of Multi Criteria Analysis (MCA) can be found in the DTLR multi-criteria analysis manual available at: http://iatools.jrc.ec.europa.eu/public/IQTool/MCA/DTLR_MCA_manual.pdf [Last accessed: 30th December 2009].

process of identifying and agreeing the investment criteria and their weightings[22] can help build consensus and commitment to the portfolio management process. Beyond this, the use of collaborative decision-making approaches such as decision conferencing to select and score projects, also helps build a shared understanding and commitment to the initiatives included within the portfolio;[23] more on this below. Some scorecards use many criteria but this implies an additional data collection burden and also runs the risk of pursuing an unobtainable degree of accuracy. The author's experience indicates that less is more and the Pareto Principle (the so called '80:20 rule') holds true. Indeed research by Cooper et al. (1999)[24] concluded that the top performers use 6.2 criteria on average. So keep it simple and focus on the most important factors – such as shown in Figure 4.1.

Some organisations include a factor relating to mandatory projects, although by definition such projects will need to be funded before any discretionary projects are prioritised. My preference is therefore to treat mandatory projects as a separate, and by definition a small, portfolio segment (although, as stated above, there needs to be checks in place to ensure that such initiatives are truly mandatory).

The assessments of 'Attractiveness' and 'Achievability' can be combined to provide a single score with which to prioritise projects but again, my preference is keep the two assessments separate and use a Portfolio Map (see sections 'Portfolio Prioritisation' in this chapter and 'Regular Portfolio-level Reviews' in Chapter 5) in informing selection and prioritisation decisions.

MCA management scorecards can be used for all projects, or alternatively, financial metrics can be used for those projects that have a financial objective (income generation or cost savings) with the management scorecard being used for all other projects, including those designed to support organisational strategy and business priorities. There is an advantage, however, in using both cost-benefit analysis, as required by the Green Book (enhanced by a financial NPV calculation as recommended above), and a MCA scorecard for all discretionary projects – the process of examining projects from more than one perspective and considering both the investment justification and achievability factors provides a more

---

22 One approach to determining portfolio weighting criteria is to use the Analytic Hierarchy Process (AHP) discussed briefly on page 62 in relation to weighting strategic priorities.

23 For more information on Decision Conferencing, see for example, Phillips, L. D. and Bana e Costa, C. A. (2007) 'Transparent Prioritization, Budgeting and Resource Allocation with Multi-criteria Decision Analysis and Decision Conferencing', *Ann Oper Res* 154, pp. 51–68. Published online: 17 May 2007, Springer Science+Business Media, LLC .

24 Cooper, R. G., Edgett, S. J. and Kleinschmidt, E. J. (1998) 'Best Practices for Managing R&D Portfolios', *Research Technology Management*, July–August 1998, pp. 20–33. Re-printed in Dye, L. D. and Pennypacker, J. S. (eds) (1999) Project Portfolio Management, CBP, Glen Mills, PA.

Factor	Factor Weight	Low	Medium-Low	Medium	Medium-High	High	Weighted score
Attractiveness		1	2	3	4	5	
Financial return							
Strategic fit							
Exploits capacity and capability							
Flexibility							
Meets specified user needs							
Attractiveness score							
Achievability		1	2	3	4	5	
Simplicity							
Planning quality							
Capacity to drive progress							
Achievability score							

Figure 4.1   Investment attractiveness and achievability scorecard

rounded appraisal. As Cooper and Edgett[25] (2006) say: '*All methods are somewhat unreliable; so consider using multiple selection methods in combination.*' This improves understanding about the nature of the investments being made, lays the basis for benefits management and helps build consensus around the portfolio for change.

Points to note about the above scorecard:

THE ATTRACTIVENESS APPRAISAL

- This includes both quantitative (financial return) and qualitative (strategic alignment or fit) factors. Financial return can be measured

25   Cooper, R. and Edgett, S. (2006) *Ten Ways to Make Better Portfolio and Project Selection Decisions*, Available at: http://www.prod-dev.com/downloads/working_papers/wp_24.pdf [Last accessed: 13th December 2008].

in terms of payback and/or NPV with scores of 1–5 relating to the size of the financial return norms for the organisation. This analysis should be based on incremental cash flows rather than attributed economic values, that is, in cases where efficiency and effectiveness benefits are non-cashable, the return shown here will be negative representing the net present cost required to 'buy' the performance improvement forecast. As noted above this does not mean that we ignore the NPV calculated using attributed monetary values as part of the cost-benefit analysis – rather we appraise potential investments through more than a single 'value lens'.

- One way of scoring for strategic alignment or 'fit' is to use the OGC definitions as shown below.

EXAMPLE 11.   THE OGC RATING FOR STRATEGIC ALIGNMENT/FIT[1]

Projects, programmes and business change initiatives can be ranked using the OGC project rating categories.

Mission Critical – Scores 5	A. ESSENTIAL to the successful delivery of: i) a major legislative requirement OR ii) a Public Service Agreement (PSA) target OR iii) a major policy initiative announced and owned by the Prime Minister (PM) or a Cabinet Minister OR B. If the programme or project is not successful there are catastrophic implications for delivery of a key public service, national security or the internal operation of a public sector operation.
Highly Desirable – Scores 3	A. IMPORTANT (but not essential) for the delivery of: i) a major legislative requirement OR ii) a PSA target OR iii) a major policy initiative announced and owned by the PM or Cabinet Minister OR B. ESSENTIAL to the successful delivery of: i) a minor legislative requirement OR ii) a high profile (but not PSA) target OR iii) other government policy initiatives OR C. If the programme or project is not successful there are serious (but not catastrophic) implications for the delivery of a key public service, national security, or the internal operation of a public sector organisation. OR D. If the programme or project is not successful there are catastrophic implications for the delivery of non-key public services or the realisation of significant business benefits.
Desirable – Scores 1	All programmes or projects that do not meet the mission critical or highly desirable criteria.

---

1   Available at: http://www.ogc.gov.uk/documents/Prioritisation_Categories.pdf [Last accessed: 9th March 2009].

Another example comes from Defra.

EXAMPLE 12.   ASSESSING STRATEGIC ALIGNMENT: THE DEFRA APPROACH[1]

Determining strategic alignment of any portfolio is ideally something which should be the result of careful deliberation and focussed challenge, particularly in an organisation responsible for the use of public resources. A quantification of the degree of strategic alignment is particularly useful when the number of activities in the portfolio is large (in Defra there are approximately 900 projects and ongoing functions). In Defra this involves scoring the expected benefits of an activity against what impact it will have on our Departmental Strategic Objectives (DSOs), the latter agreed with Her Majesty's Treasury. This is how it works. Each DSO is a strategic statement on a key area of Defra's vision and comprises several Intermediate Outcomes (IOs) which are the real world changes that will lead to realising each DSO. A particular activity's impact on all relevant IOs is averaged numerically and combined with a score on the expected net economic benefit of the activity. This combination is called a Generalised Benefit (GB) score. Activities are also scored in other ways: through their political commitment, whether or not there is a legislative or legal requirement for Defra to deliver this activity, and so on. The benefit of using such a scoring system is that it provides:

1.   a simple estimate of the strategic alignment of an activity and thus of the whole portfolio (high GB score means high strategic alignment or high net economic benefit);

2.   a means for rapidly isolating poorly aligned, high-cost activities for further scrutiny, especially in the context of identifying potential areas for realising savings;

3.   a route to estimating performance efficiency of the portfolio (GB divided by project cost is an efficiency ratio);

4.   greater transparency for key players (Senior Responsible Officers (SRO), Approval Panels, Management Board and Ministers) of the work going on in the organisation.

The main use of this approach is to inform but not substitute for judgement by the organisational leaders. The risk of relying exclusively on any numerical approach is the quality of the data required to support it. At Defra everyone involved in portfolio management is made aware of this limitation and encouraged to use this approach as a strawman for challenge of the relative importance of different activities within the portfolio rather than as an end in itself. There is also an issue of burden on staff to estimate the scores involved and validate their accuracy through processes of internal scrutiny and this cost to the business has to be counterbalanced by adequate realisation of the above benefits. In Defra, the amount of time and effort spent on this aspect of Portfolio Management is kept proportionate to the needs of the senior decision-makers.

---

1   Provided with the kind agreement of Achilleas Marvellis, Richard Price and David Cope of Defra.

Where the organisation has adopted an enterprise architecture, this can also be used to assess the degree of alignment between business strategy and the proposed initiative – both in relation to the 'as is' and the 'to be' architecture.

Where there is more than one strategic priority, the Strategic Alignment score can represent a composite score – each strategy is weighted and the project is assessed against each strategy and the scores are totaled to calculate an overall Strategic Alignment score for the project. Prioritising strategic targets can however be problematic given that there are often powerful constituencies supporting each target within the organisation. One solution is to weight them equally although a more robust approach is to use the Analytic Hierarchy Process[26] to determine relative priorities by means of pair wise comparisons – senior management discuss and rank each strategic objective, two at a time, assessing how much more important one is compared to the other on a sliding scale. The scale used by Microsoft Office Project Portfolio Server 2007 for example is as follows: 'extremely more important', 'strongly more important', 'moderately more important', 'equal', 'moderately less important', 'strongly less important', and 'extremely less important'. Where there are differences of opinion they are at least 'brought into the light' and can be discussed until resolution is reached. The results are then consolidated (usually by a software program as the mathematics can be daunting) to provide a prioritised ranking of strategic objectives. Projects are then scored against each strategy (the scale used by Microsoft Office Project Portfolio Server 2007 being for example: 'extreme', 'strong', 'moderate', 'low' or 'none') based on the contribution to the quantitative measures identified for each strategic driver. When these scores are weighted and totaled, the result is a weighted strategic value score for each project.

• The appraisal also includes an assessment of the degree to which the potential investment exploits previous investments in capacity and capability. The objective here being to credit investments that enable the value created from previous investments to be leveraged via reuse.

---

26 A useful introduction to the AHP can be found in 'Using the Analytical Hierarchy Process to Improve Enterprise Project Portfolio Management' by James Devlin in Levine, H. (2005) Project Portfolio Management, Jossey-Bass. Other than Microsoft Project Portfolio Server, software packages that incorporate AHP include Expert Choice and HIPRE 3+.

- Flexibility – as discussed in Chapter 2, active Portfolio Management is not about once and for all decisions, rather it involves managing the collection of projects, programmes and initiatives on an ongoing basis to optimise return and strategic contribution, and maintain portfolio-level balance. Flexibility therefore has a value in terms of the organisation's ability to redirect resources in the light of changed conditions. Truly modular, phased and incremental approach projects should therefore be scored more highly than those that only demonstrate a positive return when the full investment is made because they enable the organisation to flex their resource allocation as knowledge is gained. Without this flexibility, resource reallocation is difficult (and expensive!) and the benefits realised from the investment in portfolio management are likely to be limited.

- The extent to which the initiative meets a user specified need – the key issue to assess here concerns: does the project or initiative address a user-perceived need or problem and how pressing/ important is resolution to *the user*? This is important because benefits realisation is often dependent on user take-up and if the user is ambivalent about the initiative, then benefits realisation is clearly at risk. A simple analysis can be undertaken using a two dimensional matrix with:

The vertical axis measuring the importance of the need or requirement to the user using the MoSCoW framework, that is:

-   M = Must be met.

-   S = Should be met.

-   C = Could be met.

-   W = Won't have but Would like in the future.

The horizontal axis measuring the extent to which the project will meet these needs (again, as assessed *by the user*) – ranging from none to fully.

Other factors that could be considered under the 'Attractiveness' appraisal include potential impacts derived from a PEST analysis, that is, Political, Environmental, Social and Technological factors.

THE ACHIEVABILITY APPRAISAL

- The assessment should encompass three aspects of achievability – technical achievability, project deliverability and likelihood of benefits realisation.

- There are numerous approaches to assessing achievability and organisations are encouraged to select those most relevant to their environment and the types of project undertaken. Options include the OGC Risk Potential Assessment and/or Rapid Risk Check[27] under which a spreadsheet is used to calculate an overall score where 30 or less equates to low risk, 31 to 40 to medium risk, and projects with a score of 41 or more are classified as high risk. If this approach is used the scorings need to be reversed as high risk equates to low achievability. The point to stress, however, is that the criteria used and their weightings should reflect the organisational circumstances – the types of project pursued, the environmental conditions and past performance. The approach shown on the scorecard above is based on the methodology adopted by the CJS IT programme – the assessments are outlined below.

EXAMPLE 13. THE CJS IT APPROACH TO ASSESSING ACHIEVABILITY

The approach adopted by CJS IT was based on the delivery factors originally used by the Prime Ministers' Delivery Unit (PMDU) to assess progress against the Public Service Agreements (PSAs). Whilst the main factors in this model were retained, the component elements and descriptions of what good looks like were revised to reflect research into the causes of project failure and the failure to realise benefits. As such the factors considered were:

1. *Degree of Complexity* – technological innovation; historic performance; constraints on delivery; scale of organisational change; stakeholders and complexity of the delivery chain; dependencies and interdependencies on/with other projects; and additional risks.

---

27 Available at: http://www.ogc.gov.uk/introduction_to_the_resource_toolkit_tools_techniques. asp. [Last accessed: 13th August 2009].

> 2. *Quality of Planning, Performance and Benefits Management* – clarity of objectives and benefits; governance, programme and project management; and performance and benefits management.
> 3. *Capacity to Drive Progress* – understanding and structure of the programme delivery chain; engaging the delivery chain; and leadership and culture.
>
> These assessments were combined to provide an overall assessment of project achievability and benefits realisation. The three assessment schedules are included in the Appendix to this chapter.

There are also other factors such as availability of resources and the ability of the organisation to absorb the business change implied, although such factors are usually better considered at the portfolio level – and this is discussed further under the section 'Portfolio Prioritisation'.

There are two main disadvantages to the MCA scorecard approach as outlined above – one that is fairly easily rectified but the other requires an additional piece of analysis. The first problem is that whilst the scorecard can provide a ranked list of projects telling us that, for example, project A is preferred to project B, that ranking doesn't take any account of the relative cost of those projects. Thus we might prefer project A to project B but is that still the case if A costs 10 times more than B? This can be addressed by dividing the total attractiveness and achievability score by the cost of the project and then ranking projects in terms of their cost per unit of attractiveness/achievability. Alternatively projects can be ranked on a scale of attractiveness per £ invested with consideration of achievability being incorporated via a Portfolio Map (see the section 'Portfolio Prioritisation' in this chapter and 'Regular Portfolio-level Reviews' in Chapter 5). See also the examples from Defra above and the Olympic Delivery Authority below where options were appraised and then a relative 'bang for buck' assessment was made.

The second more significant problem is that unless the project demonstrates a positive financial return on investment, the scorecard doesn't tell us whether it is worth investing in the project in the first place. That is, we might prefer project A to project B but are the benefits promised by project A worth the cost – is the forecast 'strategic bang' worth the investment of our financial 'buck'? We consequently need to look beyond strategic alignment or fit, to strategic contribution – in short we need to understand *how exactly* the project will impact on the organisation's strategic priorities, *to what extent*, and *how confident* are we in the contribution claimed? Senior management will then be in a position to judge whether it is worth investing the required funds to realise the value forecast taking into consideration both the absolute and the relative benefits, that is, by considering the investment case in the context of the alternative uses to which the funding required could be put. Ultimately this will often remain an issue for management judgment – but it is better to recognise reality and to make the implicit assumptions underlying investments explicit. As outlined in Chapter 2, this can be facilitated by Strategic Contribution Analysis which combines analysis of Strategy Mapping with Benefits Mapping to provide a clear line of sight from strategy to initiative, and in turn to individual performance objectives, that is, an analysis of the investment logic chain from:

- Vision (where we are trying to get) through Strategy (how we will get there) to Success measures (how we'll know we've arrived successfully); and

- Initiative, thorough business changes required to realise the potential benefits, and their contribution to the success measures referred to above.

An interesting illustration of this approach is provided by the Investment Logic Maps developed by the Victorian State Government in Australia.

EXAMPLE 14.   VICTORIA GOVERNMENT'S INVESTMENT LOGIC MAPS[1]

At the heart of the Investment Management Standard adopted by the Victorian Government, is the Investment Logic Map which depicts the story of the investment on a single page in a form that can be easily understood and adapted to represent a changing story. It shows the:

1. drivers or the problem at hand, along with the high-level strategic interventions proposed to address the problem;
2. benefits to the organisation and its customers that result from addressing the problem (these will be supported by Key Performance Indicators (KPIs) that are meaningful, attributable and measurable); and
3. business changes and enabling assets required to realise those benefits.

The Logic Map is the output from a series of three, two-hour workshops focusing on defining the problem, the benefits sought and the likely solution – for small investments this is developed in just one workshop. Fundamental to the success

---

1   The information was provided with the kind and extensive cooperation of Terry Wright of the Victorian Department of Treasury and Finance.

of the process is the engagement of senior executives. The participants will vary between the three workshops, but will include the 'investor' (the person who has identified the business need, who will be making or advocating the decision to invest, and who will be responsible realising the benefits), along with relevant internal and external stakeholders. The crucial point is that the debate starts with the problem faced rather than seeking to justify a solution.

These are not 'once only' exercises – Investment Reviews are undertaken at specified intervals where project performance is assessed against cost and schedule and the two-hour workshop is repeated to test the continuing relevance of the investment logic. The outcome of this review is a decision by the governance body to continue, discontinue or vary the terms for implementing the investment. The Investment Logic Map and Benefits Management Plan will also be re-endorsed. The key themes underpinning the approach are:

- a clear statement relating strategic drivers to objectives and benefits, and the business and enabling changes required to realise those benefits;
- short summary documentation focusing on the key high-level benefits and the KPIs that will be used to assess benefits realisation; and
- regular investment reviews and recommitment to the investment logic and benefits management plan.

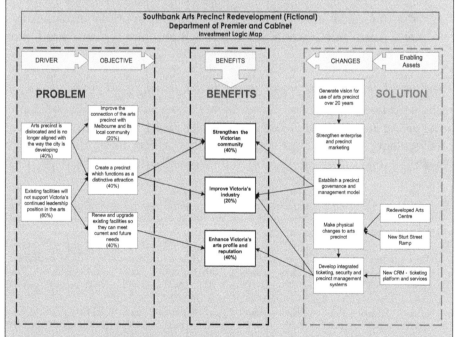

Figure 4.2   Investment logic map

The main advantages of management scorecards and MCA (particularly where they are enhanced by Strategic Contribution Analysis) are that they: recognise the importance of management judgment and take account of softer/qualitative factors; facilitate inclusion of consideration of all forms of value, quantitative and qualitative, financial and non-financial; and help build consensus around investments, particularly where decision conferencing approaches are also employed. Under the latter approach, key stakeholders attend a workshop and debate the investment criteria to be used, their weightings, the relative merits of the various options and projects, and any trade-offs required. As we shall see in a moment, such approaches have been shown to be effective – but they do depend to a great extent on effective facilitation. I have witnessed Decision Conferences that grasped the difficult issues and others that skirted them completely and the difference each time lay in the facilitator. The key attributes of an effective facilitator are the 3 I's of:

- Independence – so he or she is not associated with partisan arguments and any specific interests;

- Intelligence – so he or she has the respect of those present; and

- Informed – the facilitator needs to have an appreciation of the main issues and constraints under which portfolio decisions need to be made.

The advantages of MCA and decision conferencing approaches have been recognised in the US Federal Government's Value Measuring Methodology[28] and the Australian Federal Government's Demand and Value Assessment Methodology.[29] Perhaps most importantly, they appear to work. Research in Australia[30] found a strong correlation between measures of project portfolio

---

28 See, for example, CIO Council (2002) *Value Measuring Methodology – How-To-Guide*, Available at: http://www.cio.gov/documents/ValueMeasuring_Methodology_HowToGuide_Oct_2002.pdf [Last accessed: 14th December 2008].

29 See, for example, *E-Government Benefits Study* (April 2003) from the Australian National Office for the Information Economy (NOIE) Available at: http://www.agimo.gov.au/archive/publications_noie/2003.html [Last accessed: 30th December 2009] and *Demand and Value Assessment Methodology* (May 2004) from the AGIMO, Available at: http://www.agimo.gov.au/archive/damvam.html [Last accessed: 30th December 2009].

30 Killen, C. P., Hunt, R. A. and Kleinschmidt, E. J. (2007) *Managing the New Product Development Project Portfolio: A Review of the Literature and Empirical Evidence*, Proceedings of PICMET 2007 Portland, Oregon, Portland International Conference on Managing Engineering and Technology (PICMET) and Killen, C. P., Hunt, R. A. and Kleinschmidt, E. J. (2008) 'Project Portfolio Management for Product Innovation', *International Journal of Quality and Reliability Management*, 25:1, pp. 24–38.

management performance (maximisation of financial value; portfolio balance; and alignment with organisational strategy) and portfolio management methods, most notably strategic methods such as management scorecards and Portfolio Maps (see the section 'Portfolio Prioritisation' in this chapter and 'Regular Portfolio-level Reviews' in Chapter 5). In the US and Canada, Cooper et al. (2006) conclude[31] that financial metrics are the most common but not the best method for project selection – because data is uncertain/unreliable, financial metrics provide unfounded confidence on the robustness of the process. They therefore recommend MCA-based scoring models and find them to be correlated with improved investment decisions. This issue of data reliability is considered in a little more detail before we conclude our consideration of investment appraisal, with some observations on the balance between data-driven decision making and management judgment.

Data Reliability

Robert Cooper (2006) has said, *'The best project-selection system in the world is worthless unless the data are sound.'*[32] Unfortunately, as we have seen already (see the findings from the Mott McDonald and the Flyvbjerg et al. studies referred to above) the data on which many organisations make their investment decisions is not as reliable as is often presumed – as a representative of the Canadian Government told the OECD in 2006: *'Business cases contain assumptions masquerading as facts.'*[33]

According to research by Kahneman and Tversky (1979)[34] such forecasting errors are derived from cognitive biases in human forecasting which include a tendency to be overconfident and underestimate risk, that is, planners tend to assume that things won't go wrong. The result is what Lovallo and Kahneman (2003) refer to as *'delusional optimism'* where planners *'overestimate benefits and underestimate costs. They spin scenarios of success while overlooking the potential for*

31 Cooper, R. G., Edgett, S. J. and Kleinschmidt, E. J. (2001) *Portfolio Management for New Products*, 2nd ed, Perseus Press, Cambridge, Mass.

32 Cooper, R. G. and Edgett, S. J. (2006) *Ten Ways to Make Better Project Portfolio and Project Selection Decisions*, Available at: http://www.prod-dev.com/downloads/working_papers/wp_24.pdf [Last accessed: 13th December 2008].

33 Mornan, B. (2006) *Benefits Realization: Government of Canada Experience*, a presentation to the Organisation for Economic Co-operation and Development, E-Government Expert Meeting: Cost and Benefit Analysis Paris, France, 6 February, 2006, Available at: www.tbs-sct.gc.ca/emf-cag/outcome-resultat/benefits-avantages/benefits-avantages-eng.ppt [Last accessed: 14th December 2008].

34 Kahneman, D. and Tversky, A. (1979) 'Prospect Theory: An Analysis of Decisions Under Risk', *Econometrica*, 47:2, pp. 263–291. Cited in Flyvbjerg et al. (2002).

mistakes and miscalculations'.[35] This tendency is so common that the World Bank[36] devised a special term for it – the *'EGAP-principle'*, that is, the assumption that *'Everything-Goes-According-to-Plan'*, which of course it doesn't. One solution is to base cost and benefit estimates on what Kahneman and Tversky call, *'distributional information'*, that is, data from previous and similar projects. This is discussed further below.

But there is evidence that the causes of cost underestimation and benefit overestimation go way beyond the problems associated with forecasting an uncertain future and cognitive biases, and can relate to behavioural and organisational issues. Lin et al. (2005)[37] for example, report that 26.2 per cent of respondents to their survey in Australia admitted to regularly overstating benefits in order to get their business cases approved. Ward reports an even more depressing situation in Europe, with 38 per cent of respondents in one survey, undertaken by Cranfield University, openly admitting to overstating benefits to get funding[38] with the traditional investment appraisal process being *'seen as a ritual that must be overcome before any project can begin'*.[39] Interviews with those responsible for preparing estimates by Flyvbjerg and COWI (2004)[40] confirm this picture of deliberate misstatement in order to get projects approved – either because it's in the economic interests of those making the case, or because it is expected by the project sponsor. This reflects the conclusions of Martin Wachs (1989)[41] who identified a conflict between planning as science and as advocacy: *'The most effective planner is sometimes the one who can cloak advocacy in the guise of scientific or technical rationality…we adjust data and assumptions until we can say that the data clearly show that the preferred option is best.'* As Sharpe and Keelin comment,[42] *'Figures don't lie, but liars can figure!'*

---

35 Lovallo, D. and Kahneman, D. (2003) 'Delusions of Success – How Optimism Undermines Executives' Decisions', *Harvard Business Review*, July 2003, pp. 56–63.
36 World Bank (1994) *World Development Report 1994: Infrastructure for Development*, OUP, Oxford. Cited in Flyvbjerg et al. (2002).
37 Lin, C., Pervan, G. and McDermid, D. (2005) 'IS/IT Investment Evaluation and Benefits Realization Issues in Australia', *Journal of Research and Practice in Information Technology*, 37:3, August 2005.
38 Ward, J. (August 2006) *Delivering Value from Information Systems and Technology Investments: Learning from Success*. A report of the results of an international survey of Benefits Management Practices in 2006.
39 Peppard, J., Ward, J. and Daniel, E. (2006) Managing the Realization of Business Benefits from IT Investments, submission to *MIT Sloan Management Review*.
40 Flyvbjerg, B. in association with COWI (2004) Procedures for Dealing with Optimism Bias in Transport Planning, Available at: http://www.dft.gov.uk/pgr/regional/ltp/major/proceduresfor dealingwithopti3687?page=1 [Last accessed: 15th November 2008].
41 Wachs, M. (1989) 'When Planners Lie with Numbers', *APA Journal*, 476, Autumn.
42 Sharpe, P. and Keelin, T. (1999) 'How SmithKline Beecham Makes Better Resource-Allocation Decisions', in Dye, L. D. and Pennypacker, J. S. (eds) (1999) *Project Portfolio Management*, CBP, Glenn Mills, PA.

Unfortunately, empirical research would indicate that this is no exaggeration – Flyvbjerg et al. (2002 and 2005) concluded that the underestimation of costs and overestimation of benefits is not due to error or cognitive bias alone, but is best explained by what they term 'Strategic Misrepresentation', that is, the planned, systematic, deliberate misstatement of costs and benefits to get projects approved. In short, as Flyvbjerg et al. say, 'That is lying!'

The answer lies in a combination of five factors: spending more time up front 'doing your homework' in developing the case for investment; more reliable forecasting methodologies augmenting 'inside view' forecasts with an 'outside view'; independent review and scrutiny of the case; triangulation and validation of the investment case; and consideration of how we can adjust the organisational dynamics to incentivise the preparation of more reliable business cases – in short by greater transparency of, and accountability for, forecasts. These five factors are considered below.

1. Spending more time up front in 'doing your homework' – failing projects tend not to have brilliant business cases and by far and away the main cause of project time and cost overruns identified by the 2002 Mott MacDonald study referred to above, was an inadequate business case, that is, inadequate requirements and project scope definition. Research at Cranfield University[43] similarly found that in 113 out of 117 cases, problems could be traced back to the business case. The solution is to spend more time really understanding and validating the user requirements and bringing the Voice of the Customer into project design as well as delivery (for example, see the Draeger case study in Chapter 5). One practitioner in the private sector, Stratton (2004),[44] emphasises that it is critical that we develop a shared understanding of the problem we are trying to solve and the options open to us. This means that the business case should contain a meaningful options appraisal for meeting these requirements, including analysis of the implications of not investing (the 'do nothing' option) and a 'do minimum' option, as well as a comprehensive analysis of alternative ways of meeting these requirements. The case should also be presented clearly to all parties – Stratton argues that, *'The business case should present clear evidence and reasoning which supports the conclusions presented in terms which can be understood from a business, technical and financial perspective.'*

---

43 As reported by Professor Chris Edwards at the UK Government Benefits Forum, 20th October 2008.

44 Stratton, M. J. (2004) Business Case Development and Analysis, Proceedings of the 2004 Crystal Ball User Conference, Available at: http://www.cbpredictor.com/cbuc/2004/papers/CBUC04-Stratton.pdf [Last accessed: 19th February 2009].

The business case should also be framed around the concept of 'starting with the end in mind', that is, it should focus on the objectives of the intervention rather than seeking to justify one particular option, and include all costs required to generate the benefits claimed – too often business cases exclude key business change costs. At a fundamental level the focus should not be on 'have we identified enough benefits to justify the forecast costs?' but 'is it worth investing £x to realise the forecast benefits?'

2. *Reference class forecasting* – Kahneman and Tversky (1979) argued that cognitive biases are best adjusted for by taking 'distributional information' into account and Lovallo and Kahneman (2003)[45] suggest deriving cost estimates from a relevant reference class of past projects. This approach is based on: firstly, identifying a reference class of comparable projects; secondly, determining the distribution of results; and thirdly, deciding where on the distribution the current project should sit (and adjusting this view for optimism bias on the basis of your past performance in predicting outcomes). Such 'outside view' approaches have been found to produce more accurate forecasts, by avoiding both the cognitive and organisational biases associated with 'inside view' forecasts, and were recommended by the American Planning Association in 2005.[46] The use of reference class forecasting has been found to be particularly valuable in novel, non-routine projects (like many transformational change programmes) where the scope for 'optimism bias' and 'strategic misrepresentation' is the greatest. It does, however, depend on sufficient data on past projects being available to provide statistically representative data – an example of how tracking project data at a portfolio level can deliver added value going forward.

3. *Independent review and scrutiny* – this can be undertaken by a Portfolio Management Office or alternatively via peer review by functional experts such as representatives from finance, procurement, strategy and so on. Ayers (2007)[47] has also suggested that boards should have an '"*Advocatus Diaboli*"…*whose job it is to poke holes in pet projects. These professional "No" men could be an antidote to overconfidence bias.*' In a similar vein, Davidson Frame (1994)[48] proposed the use of '*murder boards*' – a cross-departmental panel charged with pulling a proposal

45 Lovallo, D. and Kahneman, D. (2003) 'Delusions of Success How Optimism Undermines Executives' Decisions', *Harvard Business Review*, July, pp. 57–63.
46 http://en.wikipedia.org/wiki/Reference_class_forecasting
47 Ayres, I. (2007) *Supercrunchers, Why Thinking-By-Numbers is the New Way to be Smart*, Bantam, New York.
48 Davidson Frame, J. (1994) 'Selecting Projects That Will Lead to Success', in Dye, L. D. and Pennypacker, J. S. (eds) (1999) *Project Portfolio Management*, CBP, Glen Mills, PA.

apart to '*make sure that arguments in support of project ideas do not have built into them the seeds of their own destruction'*.

In a similar vein, I[49] call for organisations to employ someone who is, as Shakespeare suggested,[50] '*wise enough to play the fool'* in challenging those assumptions that masquerade as facts. This is illustrated in Examples 15–17. But just to emphasise – challenge does not have to be a negative, points scoring exercise, rather when performed well, it can represent a highly effective 'critical friend' role.

EXAMPLE 15.   INDEPENDENT SCRUTINY IN BRITANNIA BUILDING SOCIETY'S 'REALLY BIG PROGRAMME'[1]

To support scrutiny of the programme and its suppliers, Britannia engaged the Concours Group to provide formal quality assurance reports, which were circulated to the Group and Executive Boards as well as the Steering Committee. Independent quality assurance reports built trust and confidence between senior management and the programme team, as well as alerting senior management when issues needed to be addressed; for example, the need to give the Steering Committee greater autonomy in taking decisions to change some of the Society's business processes to enable them to be supported by off-the-shelf software packages.

---

1   Sourced from: National Audit Office (17th November 2006) *Delivering Successful IT-enabled Business Change*, Available at: http://www.nao.org.uk/publications/0607/delivering_successful_it-enabl.aspx [Last accessed: 13th December 2008].

---

4. *Triangulation and validation* – linked to the above point, use more than one appraisal method, or 'value lens', to assess the business case, and validate the claims made wherever possible. Combine economic appraisal with financial appraisal of cash flows, MCA/management scorecards, and peer/functional review. Subject the results to sensitivity analysis – testing to assess the affect of changes in investment criteria weightings and scorings. This also includes agreeing the benefits forecasts with those that will be responsible for realising them BEFORE the investment is made and wherever possible, booking the benefits in budgets, targets and performance agreements.

---

49 Jenner, S. (2009) *Realising Benefits from Government ICT investments – A Fool's Errand?*, Academic Publishing International, Reading, UK. Available from www.academic-publishing.org.
50 As with Feste in Shakespeare's *Twelfth Night*.

EXAMPLE 16.   REVIEW OF BUSINESS CASES BY AN INDEPENDENT PORTFOLIO UNIT USING MULTIPLE 'VALUE LENS'

CJS IT project business cases were appraised by an independent Portfolio Management Office. Project appraisals were undertaken by trained Portfolio Analysts and included:

- attractiveness:
  - financial/economic analysis against the HM Treasury Green Book rules;
  - checking the robustness of the benefits claimed against the 'Benefits Eligibility Framework' – a set of rules that applied to all projects in the portfolio about which benefits would be counted, how they were quantified and valued;
  - agreeing benefits with the recipient organisation, efficiency planners and strategy planners.
- achievability:
  - review of the business case against the NAO/OGC common causes of project failure;
  - a self-assessment questionnaire based on the PMDU framework for assessing PSA delivery (see above and Appendix to this chapter).

These assessments were then informed and augmented using an evidence-based Investment Appraisal tool (see Example 17 below).

- affordability: availability of sufficient funding – both capital and operating expenditure.

The output of this process was a summary report highlighting the salient facts and a recommendation to the governance bodies – saving senior managers the time and effort of reviewing large documents and ensuring that all project proposals were in a common format with the same standard information.

Effective scrutiny is dependent on suitably skilled and experienced staff and having a clear baseline against which to appraise potential investments. One solution to this issue of a common baseline is the methodology outlined in Example 17.

EXAMPLE 17.   AN EVIDENCE-BASED APPRAISAL OF INVESTMENTS[1]

'Investment Analyser' and 'Portfolio Analyser' from Proving Services are decision-support tools derived from research undertaken at Cranfield University into the

---

1   Provided with the kind agreement of Karen Farquharson and Simon Wilson of Proving Services (www.provingservices.co.uk).

underlying causes of project and programme success and failure. Projects are assessed via a review of the business case and interviews with key stakeholders. The data captured is then assessed against the baseline factor sets identified by the research, but adapted to the phase of the project and organisational factors such as its strategic priorities. The output is a succinct assessment of project:

- Achievability – based on appraisal against the key research-based factor set covering issues such as: 'Clarity and Perception', 'Accuracy and Completeness', Complexity Management', 'Processes and Resources', 'Ownership and Accountability', 'Belief of Stakeholders in Achievability' and 'Dependencies'; and
- Attractiveness – when measured against the organisation's strategy, objectives and benefits required.

'Portfolio Analyser' then takes these appraisals and analyses them at the collective or portfolio level considering additional factors as dependencies, interdependencies and balanced coverage of strategic priorities.

The Proving Services toolkit has been Gold Accredited by the APMG[2] based on the use of the toolkit within the Ministry of Defence and by the CJIT Portfolio Management Office. The fact that the tools were developed from empirical research and were independently accredited helped facilitate acceptance of the process and this in turn provided a stimulus to better business cases as project teams and sponsors sought to address the weaknesses identified by the review – another example of you get what you measure.

Of course a tool is only as good as the person using it – as was pointed out in Chapter 2 – in the right hands an evidence-based tool, informing assessments of 'Attractiveness' and 'Achievability', can play a key role in improving investment appraisal and portfolio selection decisions as well as the underlying project rationale.

A new tool (Decision Foundry) and extended evaluation criteria (Helix) have now been developed to reflect current research and to provide a solution that can be tailored to different categories of project. The new evaluation set has also been developed to include those environmental factors that have been shown by research to impact on the outcome of a portfolio and its component projects.

---

2   See http://www.apmgroupltd.com/nmsruntime/saveasdialog.asp?IID=304&sID=162.

5. *The organisational dynamics for more accurate forecasting* – we have already seen that research has shown that forecasting 'errors' are often deliberate. In asking the question why this should be, Flyvbjerg et al. (2002) conclude that it is because, '*Lying pays off, or at least economic agents believe it does.*' The incentives, in the form of project funding, are to lie or at least, to quote former Cabinet

Secretary Sir Robert Armstrong,[51] to be *'economical with the truth'*, and the penalties are remote. Similarly, if the business case writer works for the project, we should be hardly surprised when business cases are developed and present a positive case for investment since they are written to justify a decision that has in effect already been made. The key questions to ask are:

- of the business case writer and business sponsor – what's your track record in forecasting costs, benefits and schedule?; and

- of the organisation – how many business cases in the last year concluded with the recommendation 'don't invest'? The answer should be more than zero – if it isn't you are either not trying hard enough to identify potential investments, or you are writing business cases to justify decisions that have effectively already been made.

Too often business cases are literally not worth the paper they are written on (and the cost incurred in developing them) – and this is a real issue when we remember the findings of the Mott McDonald and Cranfield University studies referred to above that in the majority of cases, the causes of project failure can be traced back to the business case. The answer is to:

- ensure that the business case is really owned by the business or SRO (and that means he or she should pay the business case writer and sign off the case);

- validate benefits claimed with the recipients prior to funding – and reconfirm this commitment at each stage or phase gate (see Chapter 5);

- monitor project performance against the business case and feed the results of current investments into future investment appraisals by capturing and acting on lessons learned. If business case writers and sponsors know that their forecasts will be tracked, and they will personally be required to explain variances, there is an incentive for them to ensure these forecasts are as accurate as possible;

- hold business units to account for benefits realisation; and

---

51 The term was used by the Cabinet Secretary Robert Armstrong during the *Spycatcher* trial in 1986. http://en.wikipedia.org/wiki/Economical_with_the_truth.

- consider one other factor, and that's as Flyvbjerg et al. (2008)[52] suggest in an unpublished paper: '*Institutions proposing and approving large infrastructure projects should share financial responsibility for covering cost overruns and benefit shortfalls resulting from misrepresentation and bias in forecasting, which helps align incentives.*' In this regard, see Example 9 in the previous chapter – Investment Principle number 6 in the CJS IT portfolio was that '*overspends should be borne by the relevant organisation rather than the ring-fence*' – the so-called, 'consume your own smoke' principle which helped focus people's attention on cost control since there was no central pot they could turn to if costs escalated.

We can't remove all sources of uncertainty, but we can address the organisational dynamics so that we incentivise transparency and accountability rather than continuing to accept those '*assumptions that masquerade as facts*'.

Management Judgment, Experience and Datain Decision Making

Resource allocation decisions require a healthy mix of managerial and professional judgment, based on intuition and experience, and data-driven analysis. The problem is that often the scales are too heavily weighted in favour of the former (judgment and intuition) at the expense of the latter (data and analytics). The consequences are seen in continuing examples of pet projects, investments being made without a real understanding of the 'benefits you are buying', and the absence of real post-implementation review and active seeking out of lessons learnt. A Corporate Executive Board paper,[53] on disciplined capital budgeting included the following comment from one representative CFO that, '*Business unit leaders always find a way to justify pet projects. Our CEO defines "strategic projects" as expensive projects without a business case.*' The reason this is amusing is that it is too often true.

---

52 Flyvbjerg, B., Garbuio, M. and Lovallo, D. (2008) 'Delusion and Deception in Large Infrastructure Projects Two Models for Explaining and Preventing Executive Disaster', Draft Paper for California Management Review, Special Issue on Infrastructure Meets Business. The author is indebted to Bent Flyvbjerg for providing me with a copy of draft 8.3 of this unpublished research paper.

53 CFO Executive Board Higher Education Cohort meeting (20th January 2006) Available at: http://web.mit.edu/finance/events/Research.pdf [Last accessed: 14th December 2008].

EXAMPLE 18.   WHAT BENEFITS ARE YOU BUYING?

One business case was presented with a healthy NPV, total benefits of £120m and several volumes of analysis prepared by consultants to support the benefits claimed. When converted to the summary benefits report required by the Portfolio Unit, the value of the top ten benefits was shown as *'not currently available'* – which led to the obvious question: *'If the value of the top ten benefits is not known, what is the total of £120m made up of?'* The problem was that each individual on the Programme Board assumed that since they had a large business case and several volumes of benefits analysis, someone must know what the benefits were even if they didn't individually. A false perception as it turned out.

Sanwal (2007)[54] calls for a *'move from the decibels to the data'*, that is, yes, management intuition and judgment are important, but they need to be informed by evidence. Whilst this is widely recognised, it appears that it is usually a form of medicine that is prescribed for others rather than oneself. The problem is that evidence-based, data-driven decision making is perceived as cutting across professional, expert and managerial discretion and autonomy. Ian Ayres (2007) notes[55] that some professions such as airline pilots have accepted this, although as he also notes, pilots are unusual in that their mistakes tend to have personal consequences of a scale and an immediacy that is rarely the case with other professions. For most professions and experts though, as Hammond says with regard to clinical psychologists,[56] the perception is that *'tools are used by clerks, (i.e., someone without professional training)'*.

This perception needs to change – if only because management judgment is not always as reliable a guide as we think in relation to investment appraisal. Whilst writers such as Gigerenzer and Gladwell highlight the role of expert intuition in decision making, we can also be misled by it (see for example the excellent 'Seven Seconds in the Bronx' in *Blink* by the latter author).[57] Whilst judgment and intuition clearly have a role to play, Piattelli-Palmarini (1994) concludes, *'What doesn't work is our intuition when dealing with risk and*

---

54 These comments were sourced directly from Anand Sanwal via correspondence with this author in January and February 2008 and from his book, *Optimizing Corporate Portfolio Management* (2007), John Wiley & Sons, Chichester.

55 Ayres, I. (2007) *Supercrunchers, Why Thinking-By-Numbers Is the New Way To Be Smart*, Bantam, New York.

56 Hammond, K. R. (1996) *Human Judgment and Social Policy*, pp. 137–138, cited in Ayers, I. (2007).

57 See Gigerenzer, G. (2007) *Gut Feelings*, Penguin, Allen Lane; Gladwell, M. (2005) *Blink*, Penguin, Allen Lane. 'Seven Seconds in the Bronx' is Chapter 6 in the latter.

probability.'[58] Reflecting the research findings of Kahneman and Tversky (1979) referred to above, Ayers (2007)[59] also notes that *'humans not only are prone to make biased predictions, we're also damnably overconfident about our predictions and slow to change them in the face of new evidence. In fact, these problems of bias and overconfidence become more severe the more complicated the prediction'.*

But it does not need to be so – the answer lies in recognising that data and analysis can't make the decision, but they should inform management decision making (as is also noted in Example 12 from Defra), and in particular:

- Take the steps outlined above to ensure more accurate and reliable forecasts, that is, spend more time doing your homework, use reference class forecasting, triangulate and validate forecasts, and subject proposals to independent review and scrutiny.

- Wherever possible, book the benefits in budgets, headcount targets, efficiency and strategic plans, and in personal performance agreements.

- Use Strategic Contribution Analysis to understand the forecast impact of projects on organisational performance, capacity and capability – and significantly, also the confidence we can have in these claims. Make the implicit assumptions that underpin much of investment decision making explicit.

- Track results to compare the performance to the promise, and hold people to account for performance.

- Accept that the future is uncertain, but in the absence of anything else, the past is as reliable an indicator as anything – if projects to date have failed to meet their cost and benefit targets why should the future be in any way different? The trouble is that many organisations fail to track and analyse performance and use this data to inform future decisions and to refine processes in the light of experience. Punters on the horses examine form, investors in the financial markets track share performance, so why not organisational performance in delivering projects? The good news is that some are

---

58 Piattelli-Palmarini, M. (1994) *Inevitable Illusions*, John Wiley & Sons, Inc., New York.
59 Ayres, I. (2007) *Supercrunchers, Why Thinking-By-Numbers is the New Way to be Smart*, Bantam, New York.

addressing this – the CFO Executive Board paper referred to above[60] for example, also noted that AstraZeneca maintains a database of past project performance and this is used to inform assessments of project risk. The Department for Transport has also commissioned research from Flyvbjerg and COWI to assess what adjustments should be made to address optimism bias in transport planning.[61] Questions for CEOs to ask their Portfolio Management Offices and Centres of Excellence include:

–   What exactly is our quantified performance over the last 1/3/5 years in delivering projects on time and to budget and what is our performance on benefits realisation compared to forecast? If the answer is, *'we don't track project performance'* – why not and when are we starting to?

–   How *exactly* are investment decisions informed by our track record on delivery?

–   How *exactly* have our processes been refined in the last year based on evaluation of recent project delivery performance?

•   Where judgment is required, recognition that the views of stakeholders in aggregate are often more accurate than those of a single expert. As James Surowiecki has demonstrated,[62] groups often make better estimates than individuals: *'Groups are remarkably intelligent, and are often smarter than the smartest people in them.'* Accepting this suggests that there is a role for perhaps the oldest investment appraisal tool of all – the Delphi technique – whereby consensus is sought from a panel of experts over several rounds of questioning with the results of the previous round being fed back to the panel anonymously. In this way the members of the panel are able to revise their conclusions in the light of the views of others. But what is crucial is that the group making the forecasts are diverse and independent – as Surowiecki says, *'The best collective*

60 The Corporate Executive Board, CFO Executive Board Higher Education Cohort meeting (20 January 2006), Available at: http://web.mit.edu/finance/events/Research.pdf, [Last accessed: 14th December 2008].

61 Flyvbjerg, B. in association with COWI (2004) *Procedures for Dealing with Optimism Bias in Transport Planning*, Available at: http://www.dft.gov.uk/pgr/regional/ltp/major/proceduresford ealingwithopti3687?page=1 [Last accessed: 15th November 2008].

62 Surowiecki. J. (2004) *The Wisdom of Crowds*, Abacus, London.

decisions are the product of disagreement and contest, not consensus and compromise.' 'Group think' is an ever present danger that must be guarded against.

- Following on from the above – robustly challenge the business case. The business case can actually be part of the problem in that it encourages the illusion that someone really understands the investment rationale. As suggested above, an 'Advocatus Diaboli' or 'fool' (in the sense of the jester in the medieval court as the only one present able to challenge the monarch) is required as an antidote to 'group think' by asking exactly what impact will the project have on organisational performance, capability and capacity – and on what basis are these claims made (empirical evidence, logic, gut feeling or hunch), how confident are we that this impact will be realised and how will we know, really know, that it has had this impact? The Portfolio Management Office can also play a useful role here.

Portfolio Prioritisation

Once potential and live investments have been appraised, we need to combine the analyses to determine what to invest in each portfolio segment, the overall shape and scope of the portfolio in aggregate, and a final sense check to ensure the results of the deliberations and analyses to date have resulted in the 'right' allocation of resources. A useful starting point is a Portfolio Map to view the comparative 'attractiveness' and 'achievability' of each investment against a breakeven line (see Figure 4.3) – with only projects above the attractiveness/ achievability line being eligible for funding. Where exactly this line is drawn will depend on organizationally-specific factors, but if in doubt I'd recommend making it a stretch to provide a stimulus to improving the quality of business cases – subject as always to the assessments of attractiveness and achievability being robust.

This analysis can be applied to the portfolio as a whole as well as to each segment and is a useful means of sifting out the relatively low value/low achievability projects – or taking action to improve the position.

Whilst projects above the line are eligible for funding, this is not guaranteed, at least not immediately – inclusion in the portfolio requires further analysis encompassing consideration of: affordability, opportunity costs, flexibility,

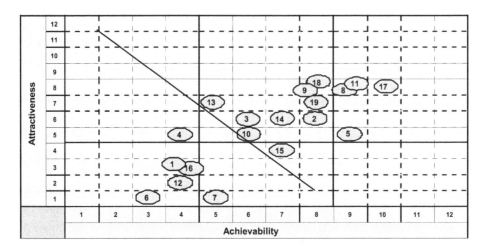

Figure 4.3   A portfolio map of attractiveness and achievability

Source: Reproduced with kind permission of Proving Services (www.provingservices.co.uk)

dependencies and interdependencies, scheduling, duplicate and overlapping projects and balance. These seven factors are considered in turn.

1. *Affordability* – both in the short and medium term, that is, we need to consider not only the up front capital costs, but also the downstream operating costs of the portfolio as a whole. Consideration of affordability also needs to take into consideration any mandatory projects since allocation of funds to discretionary investments will need to be made after these 'must do' projects are funded. But mandatory projects need to be confirmed as such, that is, the source of the mandate needs to be confirmed (legal, regulatory or political) along with an analysis of: how the project will meet the mandatory requirement; that it cannot be achieved more cost effectively; and all aspects of the project are necessary.

2. *Opportunity costs* – unless additional investment funds are freely available, all investments have an opportunity cost in that an investment decision now has implications in terms of our ability to fund other projects both now and in the future. So it is possible to have a project with a compelling business case where in the interests of the portfolio as a whole, a decision will be made to go with the 'good enough' option as opposed to the more expensive ideal solution. What is ideal for one part of the business may well not be so from the perspective of the portfolio as a whole when available funding is considered. This emphasises the point made above, that business

cases need to include a real and meaningful options analysis. An interesting example of this, and the use of MCA to prioritise between the identified options, is provided by the example from the Olympic Delivery Authority (ODA) shown below.

This issue about the opportunity cost of an investment applies both in selecting the preferred option (see example below) and when prioritising projects for inclusion in the change portfolio. There is clearly a risk that criteria and weightings might be chosen that favour one (usually more expensive) solution. The Treasury Green Book therefore suggests including *'at least one stakeholder representing the opportunities that an expensive solution would be foregone elsewhere'*.

EXAMPLE 19.   OPTIONS APPRAISAL USING MULTI CRITERIA ANALYSIS[1]

The ODA assesses options against a set of 'value categories' encompassing quantitative and qualitative factors including: Fit-for-Purpose, Time, Sustainability, Legacy, Health and Safety; Security; Equality and Diversity; Risk and Benefits. These criteria, and their weightings, were agreed with key stakeholders. Scorings are undertaken by relevant 'technical heads' or subject matter experts within the ODA which helps ensure objectivity. Dividing the value score by the cost of the option provides a value for money score which enables a relative 'bang for our buck' assessment.

---

1   This example is provided with the kind agreement of Kenna Kintrea and Ky Nichol.

---

3.   *Flexibility* – as we have already seen, a key aspect of Portfolio Management concerns our ability to reallocate funds as organisational knowledge improves and in response to changed conditions and priorities. We therefore need to assess the degree to which the portfolio can be adjusted in future to reflect changed conditions without wasting previous spend. A key feature of portfolio-level prioritisation is consequently an assessment of the extent to which initiatives in the portfolio are based on modular or incremental approaches, whereby some value can be derived from each module or phase should funding need to be cut back or rescheduled in the future. Consideration also needs to be given as to whether the full budget is allocated, or whether a portion is held back, either for new emerging ideas, or as contingency in case of cost escalation on current projects.

4.   *Dependencies and inter-dependencies* – again, Portfolio Maps (see Figures 4.3 and 5.1) are a useful means of highlighting dependencies between projects. They are particularly useful in demonstrating the value of infrastructure investments – by illustrating how relatively high-value applications are dependent on an infrastructure investment.

5.   *Scheduling* – portfolio-level investment decisions are not just 'go' or 'no go' but also concern 'when', that is, a project may well be approved, but that does not necessarily mean it will start immediately – investments need to be prioritised against others within the portfolio and may be provisionally allocated funding in a later period. So Portfolio Management concerns not just the current year but a forward look over several periods – and that encompasses planning of funding (to ensure an even investment profile), resource/skills allocation and business change commitments so that delivery is even and achievable. Retna (2004) reports that before they introduced portfolio management, projects in the AAA of Northern California, Nevada and Utah were linked to the annual budgeting cycle with consequent bottlenecks as many projects sought access to limited skilled resources at the same time. Implementing an Enterprise Portfolio Management Office (EPMO) helped address this: '*Schedules were adjusted to reflect [the] critical path and were no longer driven by annual budget cycles. The EPMO was able to work out creative solutions to resource-constraint problems. We smoothed the load on our in-house resources as much as possible and augmented them with outside resources when necessary.*'[63]

This point about scheduling, is also neatly illustrated by the following example from Booz Allen Hamilton.[64]

EXAMPLE 20.   SCHEDULING: PRIORITISATION IS NOT JUST A 'GO' OR 'NO GO' DECISION, BUT ALSO 'WHEN'

'You and four other people are stranded on an island in the middle of the ocean with no supplies: you are all desperate to return home safely. After two days a genie appears and promises that he will provide all of the following: 1. all the food

---

63 Retna, S. (2004) *Maximising Return on IT Investments With Enterprise Portfolio Management: Part 1*, *Computerworld Management*, Available at: http://www.computerworld.com/managementtopics/management/project/story/0,10801,98169,00.html [Last accessed: 19th February 2009].

64 Booz Allen Hamilton (2002) *Building a Methodology for Measuring the Value of E-Services*, Available at: http://www.estrategy.gov/documents/measuring_finalreport.pdf [Last accessed: 1st December 2008].

and water you need, 2. a radio, 3. a boat, 4. flares and 5. $10 million per person. The only condition of his generosity is that he will deliver the items one at a time at three-day intervals. How will your lucky group of castaways decide which item they want the genie to deliver first?. The castaways must decide the relative importance of each gift for reaching their ultimate objective – getting home safely. Given that goal, it is likely that they would first request food and water and, second, a boat. The other gifts offered by the genie would also be ranked so that the remainder of the schedule may be determined.'

6.   *Duplicate and overlapping projects* – are there, for example, similar projects occurring in different parts of the organisation where we could exploit synergies and achieve savings from sharing common components and processes, or by exploiting skills developed?

7.   *Balance* – is the portfolio balanced in terms of:

   • project life cycle, that is, do we have a pipeline of projects at various stages in their life cycles?

   • long-term investments, that support the creation of capability and capacity, and projects with a more immediate financial return?

   • size of investments – large, medium and small, and in terms of resource requirements and management attention required?

   • risk – is the overall risk of the portfolio acceptable in terms of attractiveness and achievability and are we overly exposed to one supplier?

   • capability – does the organisation have the skills and resources to 'land' the portfolio as a whole and are savings possible from recruitment of additional internal resources rather than relying excessively on contractors and consultants? and

   • last, but far from least, the impact on the business, that is, is the cumulative business change impact of the portfolio reasonable? The risk we face is that projects are started without adequate consideration of the organisation's capacity to absorb the change required. Benko and McFarlan (2003)[65] argue for the management of business change at a portfolio level to ensure the effective use of the *'finite resource of change capacity'*. They suggest estimating how much change capacity projects and programmes use by assessing four variables:

1.   the magnitude of the change required;

2.   the ability of the constituency to change including the ease of implementation and whether new skills are required;

3.   the willingness of the constituency to change ranging from 'resistance' to 'welcome'; and

4.   timing compared with other simultaneous requests.

What should be clear is that, even putting aside the discussion above about the role of data and analytics in appraising individual investments, when it comes to deciding the shape and scope of the portfolio as a whole, management judgment is fundamental – although the exercise of this judgment needs to be set in the context of an analysis of the above factors so enabling management to make *informed* decisions and providing a basis for the management of the portfolio on an active and ongoing basis. It is to this element of portfolio management that we turn in the next chapter.

Chapter 4 Conclusions and Take-aways

1.   Treat projects, programmes and other change initiatives as INVESTMENTS – yes focus on cost control and project delivery, but above all, focus on benefits and make the implicit assumptions underpinning all investments explicit.

2.   In appraising potential projects for investment we need to consider project attractiveness in the context of their achievability.

3.   Measures of attractiveness will depend on the purpose of the

---

65   Benko, C. and McFarlan, F. W. (2003) *Connecting the Dots*, Harvard Business School Press, Boston, Mass.

investment, that is, NPV for cashable efficiency savings and revenue enhancing investments, but for other investment objectives develop appropriate measures of value, for example, use Strategic Contribution Analysis to understand the logic behind performance-enhancing benefits, the scale of the anticipated impact and confidence that they will be realised. Where the benefits are related to staff savings, ensure realistic plans are in place to realise the time freed up for other value-adding activity – and remember, the benefit is not the cost of the time saved but the value of the work done in the time saved.

4.   In assessing attractiveness also take into consideration:

- the degree to which potential investments exploit previous investments in capacity and capability, crediting those that enable the value created from previous investments to be leveraged via reuse; and

- portfolio management is not about once and for all decisions, rather it involves managing the collection of projects, programmes and initiatives on an ongoing basis to optimise return and strategic contribution, and maintain portfolio-level balance. Flexibility therefore has a value in terms of the organisation's ability to redirect resources in the light of changed conditions – so encourage the use of modular, phased and incremental approaches to project development and implementation.

5.   Measures of achievability need to take account of technical and project deliverability as well as confidence in benefits realisation.

6.   Financial approaches are the most common approach to investment appraisal but they have several weaknesses. Firstly, they are premised on accurate estimates of costs and benefits, yet research shows estimates are often a lot less accurate than we'd like to believe – 'optimism bias' and 'strategic misrepresentation' are a reality. Secondly, they risk obscuring the real nature of the investment and its benefits particularly where the benefits are non-financial in nature. Thirdly, empirical research indicates that they can lead to poor decision making.

7.   MCA and management scorecards can help address these weaknesses (particularly when supported by Strategic Contribution Analysis) and: facilitate inclusion of consideration of all forms of value, quantitative and qualitative, financial and non-financial; can help build consensus around investments, particularly where decision conferencing is also employed, and also around the portfolio prioritisation process itself; and research indicates that they work in terms of maximising value, balancing the portfolio and improving alignment with, and more to the point, contribution to organisational strategy.

8.   The most effective investment appraisal and portfolio prioritisation approaches use more than one value lens – they triangulate appraisals by combining financial metrics with MCA and Strategic Contribution Analysis. They validate forecasts by spending more time doing their homework, augmenting 'inside view' forecasts with an 'outside view', subjecting investments to independent review and scrutiny, by booking benefits where possible, aligning personal performance agreements with project success and benefits realisation, and by tracking results and holding business units to account for realising the benefits they have committed to.

9.   Investments also need to be appraised from a portfolio-level perspective, that is, taking into account dependencies, inter-dependencies, constraints and affordability, is the overall portfolio balanced in terms of: strategic coverage; in terms of short and longer-term investments; are risks at a portfolio level acceptable; and, is it sufficiently flexible to enable funding reallocations in response to organisational learning and environmental change without significant loss of investment?

Appendix to Chapter 4 – Assessing Achievability

Assessment: Degree of Complexity			
Areas to Assess	**Example Questions**	**Best Case [Scores 5]**	**Worst Case [Scores 1]**
Technological Innovation	Is this a bespoke solution? Is there a requirement to interface to multiple legacy systems? Does the solution require innovative technology?	Off-the-shelf solution using proven technology. No or low level of integration required. Data standards and security issues addressed.	Bespoke solution using innovative technology requiring integration with multiple systems. Agreement on security and data standards required.
Historic Performance	How close is the date for project or programme completion? Has recent performance been on track?	Project close to completion; continuation of trend will deliver the project on time with relatively few changes required.	Long time span (>3 years) to project completion; a major reversal in performance trend is required.
Constraints	Are there any constraints that make the project or programme particularly difficult to deliver?	No constraints, or only a few constraints, that can be managed.	Major constraints exist that will be difficult to manage and which will significantly impact on ability to deliver.
Organisational Change	Is major organisational change required along the delivery chain in order to realise the planned benefits?	No major organisational change required and business change restricted to the home organisation.	Major organisational change required across organisational boundaries to realise the planned benefits.
Stakeholders	How complex is the delivery chain? What mix of departmental, other public body, private sector, and other agency action will be needed to ensure successful delivery?	Relatively uncomplicated/ manageable delivery chain involving few suppliers and end users.	Wide ranging and multi-organisational delivery chain that is very difficult to manage with multiple suppliers and a diverse universe of end users.
Interdependencies	How dependent is this project or programme on the delivery of other projects or change programmes?	Inter-dependencies well understood and manageable.	Several major and critical interdependencies. A number of organisations must work together to achieve planned benefits realisation.
Additional Risks	What additional risks are associated with delivering this project or programme? How great an impact could they have?	Generally low impact and probability with any higher severity risks easily manageable.	Many high-impact and high-probability risks that are difficult to manage.

Assessment: Quality of Planning, Performance & Benefits Management

Areas to Assess	Example Questions	Best Case [Scores 5]	Worst Case [Scores 1]
Clarity of Objectives and benefits	Are desired business objectives, business benefits and project success criteria clearly specified and understood?	Business objectives, business benefits and project success criteria are clearly specified, understood.	Business objectives, business benefits and project success criteria are not clearly specified.
	Are the business benefits clearly aligned with strategic priorities?	Business benefits are clearly defined and are mapped to strategic priorities in measurable terms.	Contribution of the project and benefits to strategic priorities is not clearly articulated or expressed in measurable terms.
	Is there a clear agreed project/programme plan?	Project/programme plan has been compiled, is well understood and is achievable.	Project/programme plans are incomplete or are not well understood by key stakeholders.
	Is funding in place for all key project stages?	Funding sources identified and agreed.	Significant shortfalls or uncertainties around required funding remain.
Governance, Programme and Project Management	Are key positions (e.g. Project Manager and SRO) filled by qualified staff with sufficient time to ensure successful project delivery?	Key positions are filled by individuals with a track record of successful delivery and they have sufficient time and resources to ensure successful delivery.	Staff in key project positions either lack relevant experience or have insufficient time or resources to devote to the project/ programme.
	Are the major risks to project or programme delivery and benefits realisation understood?	Key risks are identified and have responsible owners.	Definition of risk too narrowly focused, key risks to implementation and benefits realisation are overlooked.
	Is there an SRO/Board managing risks, resolving issues, tracking milestones, costs, benefits and delivery?	SRO and/or Board members are clearly accountable for outcomes and actively tackle variances.	SROs/Boards are not clearly accountable for outcomes; Boards act as discussion fora, with little decision making.

Assessment: Quality of Planning, Performance & Benefits Management			
Areas to Assess	**Example Questions**	**Best Case [Scores 5]**	**Worst Case [Scores 1]**
Performance and Benefits Management	Has a Benefits Realisation Plan (BRP) been completed and agreed?	A BRP has been documented and agreed with named benefits owners.	A BRP has not been agreed and benefits have not been agreed with the recipients.
	Have effective measures to assess take up been identified?	Measures of take-up identified and are easily collected.	No measures or indicators identified or those that have been will be difficult to collect.
	Have effective measures to assess impact been identified?	Measures of impact identified and are easily collected.	No measures or indicators identified or those that have been will be difficult to collect.
	Are project highlight reports prepared frequently covering progress against key milestones, costs, risks and identify material variances?	Good quality performance reports are produced on a regular basis.	Performance reporting is infrequent, incomplete or the information is not reliable.
	Is effective action taken to address material variances?	Prompt and effective action is taken to address emerging variances.	Variances remain unaddressed or progressively worsen.

Assessment: Capacity to Drive Progress			
Areas to Assess	**Example Questions**	**Best Case [Scores 5]**	**Worst Case [Scores 1]**
Understanding and Structure of the Project or Programme Delivery Chain	Has the structure of the delivery chain been identified?	Key stakeholders have been identified.	Key aspects of the delivery chain are not clearly understood.
	Are people throughout the project or programme working to a ranked set of priorities?	Key stakeholders are fully aware of the project/programme's priorities.	People are working on numerous and conflicting 'priorities' with no agreed ranking.
	Are there effective arrangements for transfer of best practice/ learning's (vertically and laterally)?	Effective mechanisms for the transfer of best practice and learnings are in place.	No or ineffective mechanisms for sharing learnings and best practice.

Assessment: Capacity to Drive Progress

Areas to Assess	Example Questions	Best Case [Scores 5]	Worst Case [Scores 1]
	Do key stakeholders demonstrate strong commitment to the project or programme?	Key stakeholders demonstrate strong commitment to the project or programme.	At least one group of key stakeholders appear unaware of, or hostile to, the project or programme.
Engaging the project or programme's Delivery Chain	Is there a Stakeholder communications strategy?	Stakeholder Communications Strategy is in place and is operating effectively.	Absence of effective communications with key stakeholders.
	Are end users fully aware of the implications of the project/programme on their ways of working?	End users are enthusiastic supporters of the project/ programme and the new ways of working.	End users are hostile to the project/programme or new ways of working.
	Does the SRO dedicate significant time to supporting delivery?	The SRO exhibits visible support for the project/ programme that is clear to key stakeholders throughout the delivery chain.	The SRO's support is not clearly evident to all key stakeholders.
	Are named individuals responsible for all key project/programme deliverables?	All key aspects of the project plan have clearly defined owners.	Key aspects of the project or programme have no named individual with clear responsibility for delivery.
Leadership and Culture	Are named individuals held accountable for performance?	Strong accountability (and support) regime conducive to project or programme success.	'Blame culture' where failure is only identified in retrospect.
	Does the project or programme team have access to all required project and programme management (PPM) skills and competencies?	The project team exhibit the full range of 'core' PPM skills.	Project team lack core PPM skills.

5

Key Process 3: Managing the Portfolio 'In Flight'

'Change is not only likely, it's inevitable.'

Barbara Sher

After reading this chapter you will:

- understand how the project portfolio can be managed so that it continues to represent the best use of available funds by:
    - managing the portfolio entry point;
    - project stage/phase gate reviews;
    - periodic portfolio-level reviews; and
    - regular portfolio-level progress reporting.

Introduction

If we lived in a static world we could appraise investments at an individual level and then at the portfolio level and that would be that. Fortunately or unfortunately, we live in a dynamic environment and managing the portfolio to ensure strategic alignment is maintained, returns are optimised, risks are managed effectively and that our investments in change deliver on their promises, is an active, ongoing process. Before we consider the main elements in the process, three 'stakes in the ground' – effective portfolio management is:

1. An *active rather than passive process*, that is, it focuses on continual refinement in the context of changed circumstances to refocus the portfolio and improve the chances of successful delivery of our projects and programmes. Even when no change is made this should be a conscious deliberate action.

2.   *Value driven*, that is, all decisions are based on how we can optimise the value from our investments as a whole. As we shall see in Chapter 6, Value Management is not about tracking benefits against a preset plan, or rather, it does include this, but it goes further in seeking ways in which capabilities created can be further leveraged to create additional value.

3.   Linked to the above point, it is based on *planning for success* rather than ensuring there is someone to blame when things go wrong. Yes, we need to have robust scrutiny and accountability for performance, but at the same time the emphasis should be on the future rather than the past, about the creation of value for the organisation rather than points scoring in pursuit of silo agendas, and how we can improve the probability of success – the most successful organisations are characterised by a focus on organisational learning and feeding the results of practical experience into future decision making (see Example 22 below).

The main elements of managing the portfolio 'in flight' are: managing the portfolio entry point; managing the project 'funnel' via a project phase/ stage gate process; undertaking periodic portfolio-level reviews; and regular dashboard progress reporting. We consider each of these in turn

Managing the Portfolio Entry Point

Experience shows that all the techniques and tools outlined so far will be of limited use if we do not also strictly manage the portfolio entry process. Where this does not work well, organisations find themselves with either insufficient new ideas coming through or too many – and often far, far too many. This problem is then compounded when politicised decision making means that some of these concepts and ideas are virtually impossible to kill. The consequence is a 'tunnel' rather than a 'funnel' of projects in development and delivery, and one that is stuffed full to the point that the delivery of the entire portfolio suffers from 'portfolio gridlock' – where there are insufficient resources to complete projects on time and the organisation's capability to absorb the required business change is exceeded.

The answer is to manage the process in a structured manner with a formal approval process for idea generation and investigation incorporating an initial concept screening process or 'start gate'. This ensures that all initiatives entering the change portfolio meet minimum standards of attractiveness and achievability as well as considering their impact on, and fit with, the portfolio (existing and planned) as a whole – for example, are there components, skills, processes and so on being developed elsewhere in the portfolio that could be reused here? The process is also dependent on a transparent view of the organisation's capacity to deliver, its current commitments and hence its capacity to take on additional initiatives – this enables a clear understanding of the organisation's ability to deliver new projects and informs decisions on project sequencing.

As suggested above, the reverse of too many potential projects can also arise with too few being identified and investigated. Andrew and Sirkin (2006)[1] identify two approaches to bringing a fresh perspective to bear:

- the 'scout' approach: the wider environment is scanned for ideas, although you need to have some idea of what you are looking for, and in which areas you should look; and

- the 'beacon' approach: attracting those with new ideas – in which case you need to let it be known that you welcome such ideas.

More fundamentally, organisations should engage with their staff and customers on a regular and active basis. Customer insight activity, including customer journey mapping and ethnographic research (understanding behaviour by observing users in real-life situations), and customer satisfaction measurement can provide a stimulus to new ideas and initiatives. The power of ethnographic and Voice of the Customer (VoC) research is neatly illustrated by the following example from the New Product Development area.

EXAMPLE 21.   ETHNOGRAPHIC RESEARCH: THE DESIGN OF A NEW BREATHALYSER[11]

Draeger Safety is a major German manufacturer of safety, emergency and firefighting equipment. One of their product lines is breathalyser testing devices used by police forces to test alcohol levels in suspected drunk drivers. A new product line in Europe was the goal, but the project needed direction and lacked blockbuster ideas.

---

1   From Cooper, R. G. and Edgett, S. J. (2007) *Generating Breakthrough New Product Ideas,* PDI, Canada.

---

1   Andrew, J. P. and Sirkin, H. L. (2006) *Payback,* Harvard Business School Press, Boston, Mass.

Two VoC study teams were formed and, after some training on how to do ethnographic research, the teams began their camping-out exercises in England and Sweden. In both countries, the teams spent time at police stations, conducting interviews with police officers and their supervisors. But the real learning and aha's came from their night time vigils – the camping-out exercise – where the VoC teams worked beside the police officers as they ran their night time road-spot checks on drivers. These learnings provided the key to a new product with significant competitive advantage. For example, the British VoC team soon realised how difficult a job the police officers had in maintaining order and control over a carload full of exuberant young drivers fresh from the nearby pub. The police order to the suspected drunks is always: 'Remain in the car!' The breathalyser test device is passed through the driver's window by the officer (who wears latex gloves for fear of HIV), and the driver is commanded to blow into the mouthpiece. It takes two minutes to get a full reading. Meanwhile the other officer has pulled over another car, so now there are two carloads of drunks to manage. Quite clearly, the police officers are somewhat intimidated by the task of crowd control – they're outnumbered, and many of the lads in the cars are twice the size and half the age of the officers (who incidentally do not carry guns). Note that officers never admitted to intimidation during the formal daytime interviews!

One solution the team came up with to overcome the problem of crowd control and intimidation was to speed up the process. The goal became to substantially reduce the two minute wait-time for test results that was creating the queue. And they did achieve this by developing a ten-second test device.

A second observation was that because of the dials on the UK version of the instrument, it could only be used on right-hand–side drivers in the UK. Thus, when a car from France or Germany, driving in the UK, was pulled over...the police could not conduct the test. And they had no option but to simply waive the car through. This behaviour was never revealed to their supervisors nor in the formal interviews. The solution was to design an ambidextrous testing instrument – an arm with the mouthpiece attached that could be swung over the top of the test device depending on whether a right-hand or left-hand-side drive car was pulled over.'

Source: Cooper and Edgett (2007)

Where there is a Portfolio Management Office it should be charged with maintaining a record of all feasibility and concept studies and advising the portfolio governance bodies as to whether sufficient new ideas are being initiated and whether adequate progress is being made in their development, or whether initiatives are sitting consuming resources without being progressed at a swift enough pace through the project pipeline.

Managing the Project Funnel via a Phase/Stage Gate Process

It is not only important that we manage the initial entry point into the portfolio but also that we manage projects as they pass through the project life cycle from initiation to benefits realisation via a project phase or stage gate process so that resources continue to be allocated in a cost-effective manner. The basic point is that all funding should be incremental and conditional on performance, with periodic checks at both the portfolio level (see section 'Regular portfolio-level reviews' below) and at the project level considered here. This should result in a funnel of potential opportunities and projects but the key point is that the shape of the pipeline should be that of a funnel rather than the tunnel that we see too often in practice.

Project reviews operate at the end/start of each stage/phase – but with increasing formality and scrutiny as we make bigger financial, resource and emotional commitments as our confidence in the investment case and its attractiveness and achievability grows. The latter point about emotional commitment is often overlooked but can be a real issue in practice. We face something of a paradox here – on the one hand we want stakeholders who are committed to the success of a project and on the other we don't want this commitment to blind them to emerging new evidence that affects the case, and yet, as we've seen, humans are often not very good at updating their positions to reflect new evidence as it emerges. The problem is that our commitment, that we believe to be based on a rational analysis of the situation, quickly becomes an emotional commitment that is relatively impervious to new evidence. The results are seen in inaction – a report from the NAO in early 2008[2] referred to, '*There was a consensus among the non-Executive Directors in our workshops that reallocating resources occurs too infrequently. They asserted that while senior management in departments increasingly have access to the necessary information to make this kind of decision, action is often not taken.*' Part of the reason appears to lie in the cognitive biases already mentioned, that is, the 'sunk cost' or anchoring effect – once we have made an investment there is a propensity, as Piattelli-Palmarini (1994) says, to continue to invest '*ever more on some investments that already have a long history when, should they be able to start again from scratch, they would not invest so much as a dollar*'.[3]

2   NAO (2008) *Managing Financial Resources to Deliver Better Public Services*, Available at: http://www.nao.org.uk/system_pages/search.aspx?terms=Managing+Financial+Resources+to+deliver+better+public+services [Last accessed: 14th December 2008].
3   Piattelli-Palmarini, M. (1994) *Inevitable Illusions*, John Wiley & Sons, Inc., New York.

Being aware of this helps, not least in highlighting the importance of making the right decisions as early in the pipeline as possible – killing failing and non-strategically aligned projects is a success not a failure, but only if the decision is made as early as possible. Another key defence against such optimism bias are regular phase/stage gate reviews with robust, independent scrutiny to ensure that the investment justification stills holds true and shifting the presumption so that if a project goes outside tolerance the assumption is that funding will be cut – funding may still continue, but the case for this needs to be made. This is more effective than the reverse where failure puts funding at risk, but unless positive action is taken, funding will continue. One problem seen in practice is that decision-makers are influenced to avoid killing failing and non-strategically aligned projects because of the consequent need to write off the sunk capital expenditure to the Profit & Loss account. This emphasises the advantage of early kills to minimise the impact of any write-offs, but there should also be an expectation that when a project is 'killed' the question, '*could we have stopped this project earlier?*' will be asked. This acts as a counter to avoiding taking the hard decision because of the impact of the consequent write-offs.

Many phase/stage gate systems are in use, for example:

- In the New Product Development arena, Cooper et al[4] propose a five stage, five gate process comprising the following stages – 'Scoping', 'Building the Business Case', 'Development', 'Testing and Validation', and 'Launch'. They also suggest that the first stage be preceded by a discovery phase and that the fifth stage be followed by a post-launch review. Before each of the five main stages there is a 'go/no go' gate review – 'Idea Screen', 'Second Screen', 'Go to Development', 'Go to Testing' and 'Go to Launch'. Cooper also proposes 'lite' processes for lower-risk projects where several of the stages (1 & 2 and 3 & 4 or 3, 4 & 5) can be combined with a consequent reduction in the gates employed.

- The OGC Gateway Process: Gate 0 – Strategic Assessment; Gate 1 – Business Justification; Gate 2 – Procurement Strategy; Gate 3 – Investment Decision; Gate 4 – Readiness for Service; Gate 5 – Benefits Evaluation.

---

4   Cooper, R. G., Edgett, S. J. and Kleinschmidt, E. J. (2001) *Portfolio Management for New Products*, 2nd ed, Perseus Press, Cambridge, Mass.

- Another approach is to organise the gates around the main business case approval stages, that is, Feasibility Study/Concept Case, Strategic Outline Business Case, Outline Business Case, Full Business Case and then periodic reviews say every six months.

The choice of which phase/stage gate model to use will to a great extent be dependent on the type of project and programme typical to the organisation, but let's be clear – this is not about providing confidential advice to the SRO or Business Sponsor which they can chose to implement or ignore. Too often gateway review processes are established but they don't work effectively – projects may be given a hard time but nothing is ever stopped and no funding is ever reallocated. Such gates can represent little more than an ineffective bureaucracy that only really succeeds in slowing projects down. An effective gate process, in contrast, constitutes a hard-edged review in which the SRO and senior Project or Programme Managers are expected to account for the investment to date and 'sing for their supper' in terms of continued funding. But this review is two way – the business also needs to formally recommit to the benefits case and to the changes required to realise the potential benefits (see, for example, the Victorian Investment Management Standard outlined in the previous chapter and the Britannia and Merrill Lynch examples below). The result is a common understanding of the project and commitment to what is required to make it succeed.

EXAMPLE 22. BRITANNIA BUILDING SOCIETY'S 'REALLY BIG PROGRAMME'[1] AND REGULAR RECOMMITMENT TO THE BUSINESS CASE

The NAO (2006) reported that Britannia's Group Board maintained close scrutiny of the business case's assumptions and forecast benefits via formal reviews on a six-monthly basis. These reviews took into consideration not only organisational issues but also changes in the financial markets. Prior to the Group Board review, the programme manager discussed with business managers whether the assumptions and benefits relevant to their areas needed to be updated. The outcomes were approval to any significant cost and scope changes, and recommitment to the forecast benefits by the business.

Board control was further strengthened by allocation of only a small contingency and the requirement to request Board approval for additional resources – including a meaningful appraisal of alternative options. For example, in the second half of

---

1   Sourced from: National Audit Office (17th November 2006) Delivering Successful IT-enabled Business Change.

the programme, it became apparent that to achieve the originally agreed level of integration of savings, mortgages and investment information, an additional £7 million investment would be required. The Board was given the choice to authorise this additional spend or to agree on a lower level of integration that would still leave the Society with a stable and much improved infrastructure (and a still viable business case for the programme). They chose the former.

In this way accountability is enforced *throughout* the process rather than post-implementation when the money has already been spent. These are *'gates with teeth'* and cover:

- *The backward look*: progress since the last gate review – has 'progress matched the promise', have the required actions been addressed and has spending stayed within the approved budgetary envelope?

- *The forward look*:

    - the revised forecast cost/benefit position – how attractive is the project in financial and business value terms and how reliable are the forecasts?

    - an updated assessment of achievability and identification of key issues and obstacles; and

    - what actions are required by the project and the business to improve the likelihood of success?

The outcome will be a clear (and documented) decision to 'stop/kill', 'hold' (that is, hold until funding becomes available) or 'go/continue'. If 'go/continue' – this will be subject to a clear understanding that the decision is contingent on performance. The agreed funding envelope that the project will be expected to live within until the next review will be determined, along with a statement of the deliverables that are expected, milestones and any other conditions the governance body wishes to place on the funding. If 'stop/kill' or 'hold' – checks will need to be in place to ensure that such projects are indeed stopped or put on hold (with funding being frozen). Experience shows that too often we encounter 'zombie' projects, which somehow live on, funded from local budgets despite the best efforts of governance bodies to kill them off, and 'ghost' projects that reappear long after they were apparently killed, often more than once, presumably on the basis that people will have forgotten the decisions previously reached. So ensure that the Finance Department shut the relevant cost centres.

In this way project funding is incremental, linked to performance and updated forecasts, with regular reviews to ensure the project is still on track – and just in case you think this is a level of bureaucracy that would only be contemplated by the public sector, it is instructive to look to best practice case studies from the private sector.

EXAMPLE 23.   PORTFOLIO MANAGEMENT IN THE PRIVATE SECTOR: CASE STUDIES

A Corporate Executive Board paper, 'CFO Executive Board Higher Education Cohort meeting (20 January 2006)'[1] included a presentation on disciplined capital budgeting and identified best practices including:

Schlumberger

- IT investments are segmented into four categories or segments: Innovation; Infrastructure; Mandatory; and Business Opportunity;
- a standard project business case template has been adopted to aid comparability;
- Portfolio Analysts review business case submissions and verify costs and benefits (including financial benefits and asset class-specific measures of strategic value); and
- use of a Project Management Dashboard incorporating: project status reports (schedule and cost); risk return bubble charts; analysis of spend by segment; and portfolio balance with analysis of projects by life cycle stage.

Merrill Lynch

- major projects are subject to quarterly reviews to determine ongoing funding with sponsors being required to recommit to benefits;
- Risk is reassessed based on performance to date using a 'SCORE' assessment with ratings on a scale of 1 (very high) to 5 (very low) for – **S**cope management; **C**larity of Business benefits; **O**n-time delivery; **R**emaining on project budget; **E**ngagement of business leaders; and
- *'Sponsor contracts prevent orphaned projects in cases of management change...there's no disowning or ignoring predecessors' commitments anymore. SCORE reviews get us away from our sunk cost mentality. We*

---

1   The Corporate Executive Board, CFO Executive Board Higher Education Cohort meeting (20th January 2006), Available at: http://web.mit.edu/finance/events/Research.pdf, [Last accessed: 14th December 2008].

focus less on what we've spent and more on future costs and benefits.' (Marvin Balliet, Director of Business Programs and Solutions.)

AstraZeneca

- projects are appraised in terms of strategic contribution;
- a database of past project performance is maintained to inform assessments of project risk; and
- priorities are revised in the light of changing conditions via formal reprioritisation reviews.

Effective project stage/phase reviews help prevent the funnel from becoming a tunnel and will occur at regular stages throughout the project's life cycle. But these reviews are on their own insufficient – in addition, we also need to regularly reconsider the project portfolio as a whole.

Regular Portfolio-level Reviews

Whilst the stage/phase gate reviews can check progress at a project level, we also need to periodically review the portfolio in aggregate – to ensure that it remains strategically aligned, balanced, and continues to represent the optimum 'bang' for our investment 'buck'. Where required, resource allocation should then be adjusted to reflect changed circumstances. On occasions this may mean that even successful projects are deprioritised (with a consequent change in funding profile) in the interests of the portfolio as a whole.

Effective portfolio-level reviews require senior management commitment, effective governance (see Chapter 7) and a credible and independent portfolio unit function to undertake the analyses and to advise the investment board. Whilst project stage/phase gate reviews will normally occur at intervals determined by the project life cycle, portfolio-level reviews are usually held quarterly, six-monthly or even annually – the frequency chosen will depend on the scale of change and the size of the portfolio, although for most, I would suggest that annually will not be frequent enough. The portfolio prioritisation process outlined in Chapter 4 will be repeated to assess continued portfolio balance, strategic alignment and overall attractiveness/achievability. One form of analysis that is popular is the ubiquitous '2 by 2' matrix beloved by consultants everywhere. Variations on the classic Boston Consulting Group's product portfolio matrix with its 'star', 'cash cow', 'question marks' and 'dogs' categories include Cooper et al.'s[5] categorisation for the New Product Development field (with its: 'pearls', 'bread and butter', 'oysters' and 'white elephant' project categories). Applied to the change project portfolio context, and utilising the attractiveness and achievability assessments covered above, provides us with a Portfolio Map for 'in flight' activity that can be analysed as shown in Figure 5.1.

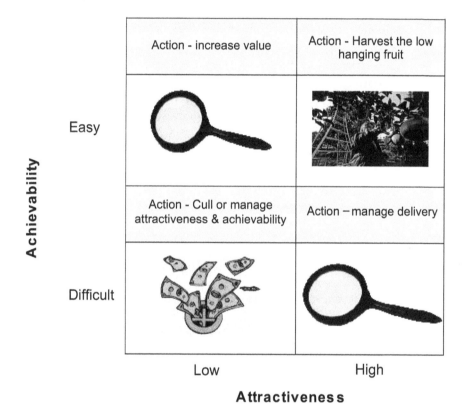

Figure 5.1   The portfolio map for 'in flight' initiatives

The advantage of this format for the Portfolio Map of 'in flight' activity is that 'Attractiveness' and 'Achievability' are not taken as givens or absolutes – rather, the focus is on what management action can be taken to:

- improve attractiveness – by reducing costs, improving benefits, reusing components and so on;

---

5   Cooper, R. G., Edgett, S. J. and Kleinschmidt, E. J. (2001) *Portfolio Management for new products*, 2nd ed, Perseus Press, Cambridge, Mass.

- improve achievability – by adopting less adventurous timescales, modular development and delivery, effective risk management, use of off-the-shelf technology, improving management of the delivery chain, effective user engagement and so on.

The portfolio-level review should monitor the effectiveness of these actions and the movement of projects over time towards the upper-right quadrant. Other issues to include in the portfolio review will include:

- The efficiency of the phase/stage gate process – how quickly are initiatives moving through the pipeline; are the appropriate decisions being taken; are we killing failing and non-strategically aligned projects early enough; is the project/opportunity pipeline sufficient in terms of numbers and quality of projects – or conversely are we risking portfolio gridlock?

- Are we producing reliable business cases – and how many recommend *'don't progress'*?

- Lessons learned from post-implementation reviews – are they being addressed effectively?

- The efficiency and effectiveness of the portfolio process itself. At least annually, the governance board should review the impact of the change portfolio, the processes used to manage it and the effectiveness of the governance process itself. Involvement by independent non-executives is advised to provide a fresh pair of eyes and fill the devil's advocate or 'fool' role referred to in the last chapter.

Performance Monitoring

The Governance Board should receive a regular (usually at least monthly) report on the portfolio, encompassing performance of the main projects and programmes and the portfolio as a whole. The objective is to provide a 'clear line of sight' from strategic intent through to benefits realisation. Production of this report often comes within the remit of the Portfolio Management Office and will include key performance indicators on:

- Major projects and programmes – position against budget, milestones achieved against those planned, benefits forecast and realised, risks and stage/phase gate results. Earned Value Analysis may also be included to link delivery progress to spend.

- Portfolio-level indicators such as – benefits realisation compared with plan; actual and forecast impact on strategic priorities; project pipeline funnel analysis including number of projects at each stage (and time at that stage); project manager utilisation; balance by segment; and key portfolio-level delivery and benefits realisation risks.

The issue of portfolio performance measurement is addressed further in Chapter 8, but single-page dashboards incorporating RAG (Red, Amber, Green) assessments are in widespread use and can provide a useful overview of current status once again, exploiting the Pareto principle. For example, the CJS IT portfolio monthly report came in five-page format with a page each for: a clear statement of progress against the desired programme end point; current year spend against budget by project; milestone progress against approved plan; current benefits forecast and benefits realised; and portfolio-level risks and issues.

These dashboards can be effective in communicating a lot of information quickly. They are, however, not without potential problems. Firstly, they risk simplifying an extremely complex delivery picture. So use them to prompt questions and to drill down to where management attention is required. A Portfolio Management Office can be useful here in directing management attention to appropriate areas for further enquiry. Secondly, there is the risk of the illusion of control – unless action is taken when required, dashboard reports are of limited value, and on the other hand there is the risk of 'micro-managing' project delivery. So use the Exception Reporting principle – highlight variances beyond tolerance for management attention and action. Where items are colour-coded red, show how long they've been red and have an escalation process when the variance is not corrected. Lastly there is the '*I don't recognise the data*' problem which results in more debate about the accuracy of the information than what it is 'saying' and what action is required. The solution is to adopt a 'one version of the truth' policy with agreed deadlines for the submission and updating data. Once again, a credible Portfolio Management function and senior management commitment to calling out any game playing is crucial.

Chapter 5 Conclusions and Take-aways

1. Things rarely go exactly to plan and conditions, and therefore business priorities, change. Consequently the portfolio needs to be managed 'in flight' to maintain strategic alignment, balance and ensure the overall level of risk remains acceptable. This process should be active, value-driven and premised on 'planning for success' with joint accountability for performance, rather than 'after the event' accountability.

2. Key elements in this process are:

   • Managing the portfolio entry point – using a structured, disciplined start gate process to ensure that on the one hand the portfolio has a stream of new ideas to investigate, but on the other, it doesn't become overwhelmed by new projects.

   • Project stage/phase gates reviews – linking funding to performance and to formal recommitment to the realisation of the benefits. Ensuring that these gates 'have teeth' so that the funnel does not become a tunnel.

   • Periodic portfolio-level reviews – monitoring the performance of the portfolio of change, ensuring continued strategic alignment, and assessing the effectiveness of the portfolio management processes themselves.

   • Regular portfolio-level progress reporting – with a bias for action so that even 'no action' is a deliberate management decision.

And remember… the object of the exercise is not to kill projects but to ensure successful delivery of projects that are strategically aligned. Yes some projects will need to be terminated either because they are no longer strategically important, or they have a low level of achievability, or because better uses for the funds have emerged – but if we have to kill projects, kill them early!

Key Process 4: Active Value Management

'The fundamental reason for beginning a programme is to realise the benefits through change. The change may be to do things differently, to do different things, or to do things that will influence others to change.'

Office for Government Commerce

'If you ask senior executives and managers as I do in my executive programmes at IMD whether their companies are extracting the expected business value of their investments in IT, the overwhelming answer by a large margin is "no"!'[1]

Professor Donald A. Marchand

After reading this chapter you will understand how:

- a focus on value can be embedded in the portfolio management processes covered in the last three chapters;
- we can go beyond passive benefits tracking to active value management.

Introduction

The key point to emphasise at this point is that benefits or value management is not something new that is added on as the final part of the Project Portfolio Management 'jigsaw', after we have established the portfolio, decided where to invest, and are managing the portfolio of projects 'in flight'. Rather, value management is something that runs through the entire portfolio management

---

1   Marchand, D. A., 'Realising the Business Value of IT: Focus on Usage, Not Just Deployment, to Optimize 'Payback', *IMD Perspectives for Managers*, 114, November 2004.

process – indeed, as illustrated by the quote from the OGC above, it is the raison d'etre of the whole approach. Consequently this will be a relatively short chapter as most of the points to note have already been made,[2] but to recap:

- *Benefits realisation as a driver for Project Portfolio Management* – one of the key drivers behind increased interest in portfolio management has been the perception of a high failure rate in terms of benefits realised compared with benefits forecast, and the potential for portfolio management to redress this (Chapter 1).

- *Benefits and developing the business case* – shift the emphasis from using business cases as a way of securing funding to a value-based document used throughout the project life cycle from selection, through control to evaluation. The focus should shift from the traditional practice of trying to find sufficient benefits to justify the cost of the investment, to asking is it worth spending £x to realise the forecast benefits? (Chapter 3). In many cases this will be a judgment call – but one in which the exercise of judgment should be underpinned by a real understanding of the benefits that will be realised from an investment. Additionally, we should look beyond hurdle rates of return where the focus is on finding enough benefits to justify the required cost of the investment, to also ask whether all potential benefits have been identified. Again, this challenge is one that the Portfolio Management Office can provide.

- *Benefits and Investment Appraisal* – potential investments are appraised in terms of their 'Attractiveness' and 'Achievability' where:

  'Attractiveness' relates to the investment justification, that is, being clear as to why the investment is being undertaken and what '*benefits you are buying*' – for example:

  - *Cashable savings* – how much will be saved in budgetary or unit cost terms and when?

---

2   Readers that wish to explore the subject of value and benefits realisation management in more detail are referred to Jenner, S. (2009) *Realising Benefits from Government ICT – A Fool's Errand*, Academic Publishing International, Reading, UK. www.academic-publishing.org.

  - *Non-cashable efficiency savings* – how much time will be saved and what exactly will this saving be used for and with what impact (and when)? This usually requires that we have adequate benefits realisation plans in place to demonstrate how time saved will be realised by redeploying staff or utilising the time freed up for some value-adding activity. To be clear – staff time savings are only a benefit when the time saved is actually redeployed to value-adding activity. Until then the time saved is only a *potential* benefit. So what conversion ratio is employed (that is, what percentage of this time saving do we assume will be converted to value-adding activity) and is this reasonable given the organisation's previous track record?

  - *Strategic impacts* – using Strategic Contribution Analysis (see Chapter 4) to understand the logic chain underpinning claims of strategic benefits including the scale of contribution to be realised, when it will be achieved, and how this will be measured.

'Achievability' concerns not just technical and project deliverability but also confidence in benefits realisation (Chapter 4).

- *Validating benefits claims* – including agreeing the benefits forecasts with those who will be responsible for realising them **BEFORE** the investment is made and, wherever possible, booking the benefits in unit budgets, efficiency plans, performance targets and individuals' performance objectives (Chapter 4). Note that where efficiency savings are booked in business unit budgets there need to be checks in place that real efficiencies are achieved and that output volume or quality are not compromised by budget cuts.

- *Project stage gates and portfolio-level reviews* – providing regular stock takes on the latest cost-benefit position to confirm that the investment case still stacks up, and culminating in a recommitment to realising the benefits by the business sponsor and those that will be responsible for the business change on which benefits realisation is dependent (Chapter 5).

- *Portfolio progress reporting* – including tracking benefits realisation against plan/forecast (Chapter 5).

So value-led Project Portfolio Management has at its heart, a focus on benefits that runs throughout the portfolio management process and this in turn requires that we establish a benefits framework as part of our Portfolio Management guidelines and procedures. An example of how a portfolio-level approach to Benefits Management can be applied is shown below.

EXAMPLE 24.　A STANDARDISED APPROACH TO BENEFITS REALISATION AT A PORTFOLIO LEVEL: THE DFPNI APPROACH[1]

The Department of Finance and Personnel in Northern Ireland (DFPNI) has recognised that a standardised, consistent approach to benefits management offers advantages in that:

- good practice can be shared;
- benefits can be aggregated and reported across the portfolio of change; and
- duplication of effort is avoided.

The approach is applied to Civil Service (NICS) Reform projects and programmes across the Northern Ireland Civil Service encompassing 11 Departments. A set of 30 prioritised core benefits have been identified, although the framework is flexible enough to accommodate additional benefits identified at departmental level. The core benefits are classified into two types – satisfaction (increased customer satisfaction and improved compliance with legislative requirements, for example) and cost. Benefits are captured at both departmental and NICS level and tracking and reporting is aided by the development of a Benefits Reporting Tool which provides a single repository for data on benefits forecasts and realisation.

The Public Accounts Committee commended this approach in 2009 commenting, *'The Committee acknowledges the work currently being completed to identify the full range of benefits that can be realised from these projects as they are rolled out over the next decade and beyond.'*

1　Sourced from a presentation by Ray Wright to the APM Benefits Management SIG on 31 March 2009 (http://www.apm.org.uk/Benefits/page.asp?categoryID=10&subCategoryID=243&pageID=0) and subsequent conversations with colleagues in the NICS.

This Portfolio Benefits Management framework should also include guidance on the classification, quantification, valuation and validation of benefits to be applied across the change portfolio enabling actual and potential investments to be consistently evaluated on a level playing field. In this way we can start to address the issues of optimism bias and strategic misrepresentation discussed in Chapter 4. Other aspects that should be addressed in the Portfolio Benefits Management Framework include the arrangements for: standard approaches to Benefits Mapping; agreeing appropriate measures and indicators especially in relation to strategic contribution; completing Benefits Profiles and Benefits Realisation Plans; revalidating benefits forecasts at each gate review; tracking and reporting benefits; and undertaking post-implementation reviews.

But we can go beyond accurate forecasting and tracking benefits realisation against those forecasts. Active value management is not just about passive reporting of benefits, but the dynamic seeking out of value – exploiting and leveraging investments and knowledge to create additional value. This is more than semantics and represents a significant shift from the traditional approach to benefits management which takes a project or programme-centric view and tracks benefits against business case forecast. The problems we face with this traditional approach are that firstly, projects don't realise benefits, the business does, and the people charged with benefits realisation, including the SRO/Business Sponsor, are often long gone by the time benefits are due for realisation. Secondly, benefits realisation is usually dependent on business change which is often not funded in the project business case (or to the extent that it is recognised, insufficient funding is allocated). Thirdly, it is difficult for anyone to get enthused by an approach that is based on passive tracking and reporting of benefits realised against forecast – which leads to the common request, *'when can we stop tracking?'* If you hear this question it's a red flag that your approach to benefits management is passive and backward looking, rather than active and forward looking. Most fundamentally the traditional approach doesn't work – as seen regularly in reports that track and report benefits down and down and down.

The issue we face is that there is no perceived benefit to anyone from managing benefits post-deployment – the project team is long gone and if the business unit identifies additional benefits beyond those forecast, it merely invites further budget cuts. Benefits management thus becomes at best an irrelevancy and, at worst, a bureaucratic overhead that focuses on appearance manipulation with glossy reports and claims of 'better', 'easier' and 'faster' but which lack any real substance or quantified impact.

The solution is to shift the focus from individual projects and programmes to the portfolio as a whole, and from backward tracking of benefits to a forward-looking perspective on exploiting the accumulated investment in change.

This approach encompasses three main aspects.

1. *Benefits Realisation Planning from an enterprise or portfolio perspective* – that is, asking the question, *'what benefits will the organisation realise this year from our accumulated investment in change?'* This can be captured in a simple report once again exploiting the Pareto Principle by focusing on the main benefits and addressing – what are the key benefits we should realise in the period ahead; who is responsible for their realisation; and what measures and indicators will be used to assess realisation? Progress should then be tracked and reported against the Portfolio Benefits Realisation Plan – but this is not a historical plan prepared prior to funding, but rather a regularly updated plan focusing on the benefits to be realised in the current and forthcoming planning period. This helps maintain a clear line of sight from strategic intent to benefits realisation as we are able to see in one view the combined forecast impact – financial and strategic – on the organisation of the accumulated investment in change. It also provides an up-to-date baseline against which to assess benefits realisation. An added advantage of a portfolio approach to benefits management is that it helps identify double counting – more than one project may claim a benefit, but they can usually only be realised once!

2. *User engagement, engagement, engagement* – the issue is not that benefits are not present, but rather that they are often not where was originally anticipated – the user finds ways to derive value that were not envisaged in the business case. The problem is that if we do not actively seek this out we have no way of ensuring lessons learned are disseminated and shared, and potential value just drifts away. The role of the Portfolio Benefits Manager is therefore not to sit in front of their PC compiling benefits tracking reports, but to get out of the office and engage with the users, finding out what benefits have been realised and what further benefits can be achieved. In this way we bring the 'Voice of the Customer' into benefits realisation. The key question to ask any benefits manager is: what additional benefits have been realised in the last six months that would not have been realised if you didn't exist?

3. *A forward-looking perspective that starts with the question: 'Is that the best we can do?'* – as always this starts from the top with leadership

demonstrating a commitment to the continual search for value and embedding new standards of expected behaviour. It also means realigning the reward and recognition strategies to align with value creation and going beyond project forecasts to realise benefits that were not recognised in the project business case and to consider synergies between projects. For example, it may well be difficult to realise time savings from a single project where they equate to, say, one-tenth of a person's time, but when we combine these with time savings from other projects this often identifies opportunities to redeploy resources. Finally, it means undertaking meaningful Post-Implementation Reviews that focus on identifying learnings that can be fed back into the portfolio management process and so influence future investment decisions and improve the portfolio management process itself. All business cases should identify what lessons have been learnt from past experience and what mitigating actions have been taken to minimise the risks of a reoccurrence.

In all the above, the Portfolio Management Office can play a crucial role by challenging benefits forecasts (to ensure both that forecasts are robust and that all material benefits have been included), analysing benefits reports, supporting business units in tracking benefits and in capturing and disseminating lessons learned. In the most mature cases this will constitute a Value Management Office (VMO)[3] function that is able to justify its existence in terms of demonstrable additional benefits realised and value created.

Chapter 6 Conclusions and Take-aways

1. Benefits realisation starts with the business case – research shows that failing programmes rarely have strong business cases. Optimism bias and strategic misrepresentation are a reality proven by practical experience and empirical research – so ensure benefit claims are:

    • *Robust* – by checking that they are consistent with the organisation's guidelines for quantifying and valuing benefits. Challenge the assumptions that masquerade as facts; and

---

3 Credit here to John Thorp for the original concept of a VMO as outlined in his '*The Information Paradox*'.

- *Realisable* – by agreeing them with the recipients prior to funding.

2. Benefits must be placed at the centre of the Portfolio Management and Investment Appraisal processes – funding should be linked to benefits forecasts and project sponsors should be able to answer the question *'what benefits am I buying?'* Project gate and portfolio-level reviews should re-baseline the benefits case and culminate in a formal recommitment to benefits realisation.

3. Wherever possible 'book' the benefits by adjusting unit budgets, reducing target unit costs, including them in headcount reductions, or by reflecting them in the organisation's and individuals' performance targets. But also check that efficiencies are real and that output and service quality does not suffer due to the creation of unfunded pressures.

4. Look beyond realising forecast benefits to value creation – benefits are usually dependent on business change and may not be realised until after project deployment has been completed and the project team has disbanded. So plan and manage benefits realisation from a portfolio rather than a project perspective; engage with users to capture and disseminate lessons learned; continually ask *'is that the best we can do?'* and challenge managers to identify additional sources of value from the accumulated investment in change.

Implementing and Sustaining Progress

'It must be considered that there is nothing more difficult to carry out, nor more doubtful of success, nor more dangerous to handle, than to initiate a new order of things. For the reformer has enemies in all those who profit by the old order, and only lukewarm defenders in all those who would profit by the new order, this lukewarmness arising partly from fear of their adversaries, who have the laws in their favour; and partly from the incredulity of mankind, who do not truly believe in anything new until they have had actual experience of it. Thus it arises that on every opportunity for attacking the reformer, his opponents do so with the zeal of partisans, the others only defend him half-heartedly, so that between them he runs great danger.'

Machiavelli, The Prince

After reading this chapter you will:

- understand strategies that have been used to successfully implement Portfolio Management in practice and the factors on which sustaining progress depends;
- recognise that whilst repeatable processes are important they are not enough on their own – we also need effective governance and appropriate behaviours if the full potential benefits of Project Portfolio Management are to be realised.

Introduction

The highest levels of Project Portfolio Management maturity represent a changed mindset in which projects don't end until benefits are realised, project and asset portfolios are proactively managed, investment decisions are business-led, and are informed by the outcomes of previous projects. The good news is that if this can be achieved then significant benefits are realisable. The bad news is that it can take a considerable time and significant effort – one organisation regularly identified as being 'ahead of the curve' is Harrah Entertainment, the world's largest gaming company. According to Jeffery and Leliveld[1] at MIT, Harrah are reaping the benefits of reaching the *'synchronized level'* with: robust business cases; clarity on business benefits expected; rigorous analysis tailored to project cost; and *'after-action program reviews'*. Their approach of 'structured flexibility' includes:

- a core Portfolio Management Office supported by governance teams from the business units. Only projects that exceed a $250k threshold are referred to a corporate capital committee;

- the Portfolio Management Office's role includes providing advice to business case writers on the selection of metrics that can be used to track project performance;

- portfolio management reporting based on *'one integrated version of the truth'*.[2]

It is however instructive to note that according to Bonham (2005)[3] it took Harrah seven years to develop their system and a project portfolio management culture. So, achieving the benefits of a mature portfolio management approach is no overnight exercise, but the challenge is eased by adopting an appropriate approach to implementation and learning to walk before you try to run.

Implementation and Sustaining Progress

Whilst one might hope that implementation of portfolio management might be driven by a recognition of the potential benefits from a more strategically aligned portfolio and more effective risk management, in practice we find that most implementations are driven by a need to address a problem – whether it be reduced funding, failing projects or a legislative requirement as is the case with the Clinger-Cohen Act in the United States which requires that government IT investments *'reflect a portfolio management approach where decisions on whether to invest are based on potential return, and decisions to terminate or make additional*

---

1   Jeffery, M. and Leliveld, I. (2004) 'Best Practices in IT Portfolio Management', *MIT Sloan Management Review*, Spring 2004, 45: 3, pp. 41–49.

2   Heath Daughtrey, Vice President of IT Services, quoted in Bonham (2005).

3   Bonham, S. (2005) *IT Project Portfolio Management*, Artech House, Inc., Norwood, MA.

investments are based on performance much like an investment broker is measured and rewarded based on managing risk and achieving results'.

Whatever the driver, sustaining progress can be problematic – initial achievements are often followed by 'backsliding' as portfolio management is seen as imposing a little too much restriction on the freedom of manoeuvre of both functional and business managers.

So where to start and how do we sustain progress? Researchers from London and Ashridge Business Schools[4] found that the four main factors identified by respondents to their survey as having the greatest impact were: a centralised inventory of all projects; clear alignment with business strategy; standardisation of project data and analysis; and consideration of project interdependencies. Beyond this, successful implementation of project portfolio management is usually dependent on the four prerequisites identified in Chapter 2: senior management commitment; a clearly articulated corporate strategy; a suitably skilled and independent portfolio analysis function; and modular or incremental project planning. To these factors we can add three additional considerations that can ease the implementation process:

1. Phased implementation – start with sub-portfolios and pursue quick wins to demonstrate the value of project portfolio management. A crucial first step is usually to obtain visibility of spend across the portfolio and then as the value of portfolio management is demonstrated, so the approach is extended in terms of expanding the scope of the portfolio and adopting more sophisticated techniques.

2. Building on existing processes and aligning portfolio management processes with the organisation's existing strategic and business planning, budgeting and resource allocation, and performance management processes.

3. A sustained training programme that differentiates between project and programme management on the one hand, and portfolio management on the other.

---

4   Reyck, B. D., Grushka-Cockayne, Y., Lockett, M., Calderini, S. R., Moura, M. and Sloper, A. (2005) 'The Impact of Project Portfolio Management on Information Technology Projects', *International Journal of Project Management*, 23: February 2005, pp. 524–537.

EXAMPLE 25.   A PHASED APPROACH TO IMPLEMENTATION: MANCHESTER CITY COUNCIL[1]

Manchester City Council adopted a four-phase strategy for the implementation of what is termed the 'Manchester Method'.

Phase 1

- Promote cultural change through the introduction of a standard method for project delivery encompassing change, service and product based projects and programmes.
- Documenting the approach in a Project Management Handbook including document templates and establishing sources of help and support.
- Training staff – to date over 800 members of staff have attended the courses developed.

Phase 2

- Improve project scrutiny through the introduction of an internal Gateway process from project mandate to financial completion. The gates include appraisals of Strategic Fit (Gate 1) and a detailed bid appraisal scrutiny panel (Gate 3). Each gate is 'owned' by a senior sponsor.

Phase 3

- Automation of the process to provide visibility and control, and to support collaborative working. The system will also enable consolidated reporting at project, programme and portfolio levels supporting 'one version of the truth'.

Phase 4

- Establishing a centre of excellence for project and programme management – building internal capacity in project management and so reducing dependency on consultancy support.

---

1   This case study was provided with the kind agreement of Kevin Fletcher, Manchester City Council and is based on the published Case Study (2007) *Addressing the Challenges of Project and Programme Management*, Improvement and Development Agency, February. Available at: http://www.idea.gov.uk/idk/aio/6056175 [Last accessed 5th March 2009].

In a way implementation is relatively straightforward – sustaining progress is the real challenge, although experience indicates that it can be facilitated by the following:

- Development of *repeatable* processes – embedding portfolio management means establishing it as part of the normal way business is conducted in the organisation. I was critical in Chapter 2 about claims that software tools are a prerequisite for portfolio management, but automation of the process can play a useful role in embedding processes. Either way, repeating the process helps establish project portfolio management as part of the corporate routine.

- As stated above under implementation – integrating portfolio management processes into the organisation's existing planning, budgeting, resource allocation and performance reporting systems.

- Continuity in staffing and an organisational 'champion' dedicated to making it happen and able to maintain momentum – implementing Project Portfolio Management is a change programme and success is greatly assisted by continuity in key roles otherwise we risk it being seen as the last manager's initiative.

- A Portfolio Management Office that operates, maintains and updates the portfolio management processes in the light of experience.

- An ongoing programme of training that overcomes the problem of staff turnover.

The process of planning and measuring progress in both process and performance terms can also play a key role in embedding portfolio management as business as usual and we will review this in the next chapter. But before that we need to recognise that implementing and sustaining an effective portfolio management approach is more than a set of tools, techniques and repeatable processes – unless decisions are made and action is taken in terms of allocating and reallocating resources in response to new information becoming available, portfolio management will be little more than an additional form of bureaucracy with the illusion of control. If we are to deliver the full potential benefits of Project Portfolio Management, we therefore need to look beyond processes to the dimensions of active governance and appropriate behaviours.

Active Governance

Research by Cooper (2006)[5] has found that in the area of New Product Development, the difference between the winners and losers is often not so

5   Cooper, R. (2006) *From Experience: The Invisible Success Factors in Product Innovation,* Working Paper No. 19, The Product Development Institute.

much that the latter don't engage in effective portfolio management but rather that they don't do it consistently. Research in the area of Information Technology Portfolio Management has reached similar conclusions – Weill and Woodham (2002)[6] and Weill and Ross (2004)[7] at MIT report that an effective governance structure is the most important predictor of realising value from IT – and the best indicator of top governance performance is the ability of senior managers to describe the governance framework. Research in the United States Government (2002)[8] also concluded that, '*Large private organizations such as GE Global eXchange Services, Oracle and Lockheed Martin noted that having a governance structure that is well documented, effectively communicated, and understood throughout an organization is critical in implementing portfolio management.*'

This governance framework will be tailored to the organisational circumstances and should address:

- what decisions are made and, in particular, those relating to resource allocation and reallocation;

- who has a seat at the table and contributes to investment selection and portfolio prioritisation decisions; and

- the basis on which decisions are made – what investment criteria are used and how management judgment (and more to the point, whose judgment) is allied to the utilisation of data-driven analysis.

EXAMPLE 26.   LINKING PORTFOLIO AND RESOURCE ALLOCATION DECISIONS

All organisations have a project portfolio even if they don't manage it as such and the point at which strategy is operationalised is when funds are allocated to projects. A key to effective Project Portfolio Management is therefore to integrate portfolio decisions with the resource allocation process. The CJS IT approach was built around a 'ring-fenced' budget which meant that resource allocation and portfolio management functions were inextricably linked.

---

6   Weill, P. and Woodham, R. (2002) *Don't Just Lead, Govern: Implementing Effective IT Governance*, MIT Sloan, Center for Information Systems Research (CISR), Working Paper #326, April.

7   Weill, P. and Ross, J. W. (2004) *IT Governance How Top Performers Manage IT Decision Rights for Superior Results*, Harvard Business School Press, Boston, Mass.

8   Best Practices Committee of the Federal CIO Council (March 2002) *Summary of First Practices and Lessons* Learned in Information Technology Portfolio Management, Available at: http://www.cio.gov/documents/BPC_portfolio_final.pdf [Last accessed: 14th December 2008].

But we can go beyond integrating portfolio governance with the resource allocation process, to align it with the wider organisational governance framework. An example of this is provided by Defra.

EXAMPLE 27.   INTEGRATING PORTFOLIO AND ORGANISATIONAL GOVERNANCE: THE DEFRA MANAGEMENT MODEL[1]

In response to an ever-increasing need for the public sector to demonstrate the value it is delivering for public money, Defra has adopted a new management model which is unique to government. This management model brings together the dual aspects of portfolio performance management – financial management and outcome performance management. The model has four underpinning components:

1.   The financial budget of the Department is fully delegated to SROs through *Delegated Authority Documents* (which include a list of desired SRO behaviours and detailed budgets) signed by Defra's Permanent Secretary.
2.   Directors General (who are executive members of the Management Board) have a policy focus but *no financial budget*. This allows our Directors General to act corporately and make the best decisions for Defra, not just for their particular policy areas.
3.   A formal *policy cycle* sets out what is expected of policy managers. Adhering to it helps policy makers focus on clear outcomes; to use evidence and to be innovative in identifying options which deliver those outcomes; to make the case clearly and robustly for what we do; and to manage risks.
4.   Staff no longer work for standing Divisions or Directorates but are part of a Defra *flexible staff pool*. People advertise their skills and programmes advertise the roles they need filled. The process gives Defra the flexibility to match the deployment of our staff to opportunities and priorities and gives our people choice with the opportunity to stretch their skills and experience.

How this works is that as programmes either start or move to the next key stage of development on the policy cycle, resources and approvals for carrying on become the subject of *Local Approval Panels* which feed into the *Central Approval Panel*, made up of Directors General supplemented by the Central Finance Director and the Chief Economist. The Local Approval Panels are similar committees at the policy Group level, chaired by a Director General, the Group Head of Finance and SROs within the Group.

The disciplines of programme and project management which underlie portfolio management are reinforced throughout Defra by the work of an *Assurance Team*.

---

1   Provided with the kind agreement of Achilleas Marvellis, Richard Price and David Cope of Defra.

This team ensures that all existing and new activities prepare detailed *Business Cases*. Portfolio management, namely ensuring that activities continue to align with the Department's strategy, is centrally coordinated through the *Corporate Portfolio & Performance Team* in conjunction with local *Portfolio Management Teams*. Both teams support the Approval Panels directly. Ensuring that resources are used to maximum effect as external circumstances change is the work of the *Flexible Staff Resourcing Team*.

The characteristics of effective governance are:

1. *Direct and active involvement of senior leaders* – to ensure decisions are made at the appropriate time and in the interests of the organisation as a whole. Those attending Boards need to be empowered to act and make decisions without referring issues back for further consideration. One key lesson learned is that when projects are killed, most recognise they should have been stopped earlier and, in practice, failing projects often limp on and on and on, consuming more resources and management attention. As stated above, project kills are not a sign of failure but of success – but only if they occur promptly. To emphasise the point – yes 'kill the dogs', but more importantly, also 'neuter the bitch'! In short, take action to cut off the supply line of poorly designed projects at source.

2. *Active engagement of business executives in projects from the start* – we don't invest in change to keep our project and programme managers occupied, but for the business benefits those investments will deliver and enable. This is why the project and programme management literature calls for stakeholder engagement, but what we are talking about here is more than just regular communication until the project is completed and handed over to the business. Leading academics in the field of deriving value from IT projects and programmes are of one voice on this. Remenyi et al. (2004)[9] call for a shift in the '*locus of responsibility for the success of the information system and put it squarely where it should be, with the line managers and user-owners*'.

    Research undertaken by Donald Marchand at IMD shows that IT can deliver business value but the key is *usage* not deployment. He

9   Remenyi, D., Money, A. and Sherwood-Smith, M., with Irani, Z. (2004) *The Effective Measurement and Management of IT Costs and Benefits*, 2nd ed, Computer Weekly Professional Series, Elsevier Butterworth Heinemann, Oxford.

argues that whilst organisations devote 90 per cent of their efforts to deployment, this only accounts for 25 per cent of the business value of IT, and relatively little effort is directed at realising the 75 per cent of value that derives from increased usage of information by managers, staff, customers/clients and suppliers.[10] So whilst selecting the right projects and implementing them efficiently is important, it is crucial that there is also a focus on effective usage of the IT and information provided – and this calls for users to be actively involved (not just consulted) from the start of the project. Professor Marchand emphasises that really exploiting the potential inherent in IT requires proactive involvement of both senior IT and senior Business Managers. Without the latter we have IT pushing a solution and without the former, the result is seen in business units pursuing uncoordinated investments.

There are, however, real obstacles to a meaningful dialogue – Jeffery and Leliveld (2004)[11] at MIT found that the absence of a serious debate between IT and business leaders was one of the main barriers to implementation of Project Portfolio Management. The problem was found to reside on both sides with some CIOs thinking that keeping business executives *'technologically uninformed translated to job security and thus took little initiative to bridge the divide'*. On the other hand, some business executives felt that a centralised portfolio management process compromised their budgetary ownership – limiting *'their flexibility, their independence, their freedom'*.

John Ward at Cranfield University (2006) has identified another barrier to real engagement: *'The data also indicates that organizations have undue faith in the business cases and that the deployment of formal methodologies gives managers a false sense of security, and perhaps an excuse for not becoming sufficiently involved.'*[12]

What is clear is that such barriers to involvement need to be overcome if organisations are to achieve the full potential return

---

10 Marchand, D. A. (2004) 'Extracting the Business Value of IT: It is Usage, Not Just Deployment that Counts!', *Capco Institute Journal of Financial Transformation*, Issue 11, August 2004, p. 127.

11 Jeffery, M. and Leliveld, I. (2004) 'Best Practices in IT Portfolio Management', *MIT Sloan Management Review*, Spring 2004, 45:3, pp. 41–49.

12 Ward, J. (August 2006) *Delivering Value from Information Systems and Technology Investments: Learning from success*. A report of the results of an international survey of Benefits Management Practices in 2006.

from their investments – and this again takes us back to the issue of leadership: in removing organisational obstacles, revising systems of accountability, communicating clearly and consistently, and personally demonstrating commitment to new standards of behaviour that encompass active involvement in the change programme.

Consider also for a moment, the background and experience of many senior executive managers and the all too often refrain, '*I don't understand all this IT stuff.*' Yes, senior managers need to better understand the role of IS/IT, but there is also a responsibility on IS/IT, project and programme staff to talk in business terms – the focus of project documentation should be on the business needs that will be met (in measurable terms) and the business benefits that will be realised.

3. *Exceptions from the process require formal approval* – data and analyses are important but Project Portfolio Management is as much an art as a science and thus calls for the exercise of management judgment. Analyses therefore need to be used intelligently to inform management decisions rather than acting as a straight-jacket on them. This does not mean however that processes are bypassed at a whim. Agreed processes need to be adhered to, with exceptions being formally sanctioned at the appropriate level and according to an agreed exceptions process. The rationale for such decisions should also be recorded and communicated to all those involved.

4. *Recognition that we operate in an imperfect world* – our models of decision making tend to assume a degree of rationality that is not always evident in practice. Research by Cyert and March (1992) for example, on the '*logic of appropriateness*'[13] and Herbert Simon's research into '*bounded rationality*' and '*satisficing*' (1991) in organisational decision making,[14] emphasise that decisions are often guided by considerations of what is 'good enough' as opposed to what is optimal. In a more recent study, Christiansen and Varnes (2008)[15] report how portfolio decision making is '*shaped and moulded through appropriate decision making rather than by following the normative calculative approach. In practice, the decision maker*

13 Cyert, R. M. and March, J. G. (1992) *A Behavioral Theory of the Firm*, Blackwell Publishers, Malden, Mass.
14 Simon, H. A. (1991) 'Bounded Rationality and Organizational Learning', *Organization Science*, 2: 1, Special Issue: Organizational Learning: Papers in Honor of (and by) James G. March (1991), pp. 125–134.
15 Christiansen, J. K. and Varnes, C. (2008) 'From Models to Practice: Decision Making at Portfolio 'Meetings', *International Journal of Quality and Reliability Management*, 25:1, pp. 87–101.

must deal with multiple factors and criteria that make it difficult to carry out a traditional rational decision-making process. Still the functions of decision making meetings can extend beyond decision-making. They may also serve as social occasions and as occasions for interpreting possible actions and sharing that information, making it possible to make appropriate decisions. Decisions are thus a construct rather than a calculative outcome'. Whilst we need to recognise this reality, and the fact that much of the information on which decisions are based will necessarily be incomplete, we can still manage the process so that 'good enough' is as good as can be achieved – not least by ensuring judgment and intuition are more equally balanced by data and analysis as discussed in Chapter 4.

5.   *Active rather than passive governance* – with an emphasis on planning for success rather than detecting failure and attributing blame. What I mean by this is that the focus of governance bodies should be on:

- an active search for initiatives to exploit organisational capacities in pursuit of strategic objectives, rather than on saying 'yes' or 'no' (and often in practice 'maybe') to projects as they present their cases. Retna (2004)[16] emphasises that *'programs must be actively managed, and the portfolio management office must be seen inside the organization as change agents and contributors capable of acting as "conductors" who help teams meet corporate goals – not as just overseers relegated to reporting and reviewing schedules';* and

- combining robust scrutiny and challenge with support to ensure organisational impediments to delivery are removed.

Whilst strong governance is crucial to effective portfolio management, Weill and Ross (2004) also report that having the appropriate governance mechanisms is not enough: *'We heard a number of horror stories about mechanisms being ineffective. For example, a common complaint was that senior executives would agree to serve on committees but would not attend meetings or would send lower-level nominees who didn't want to make hard decisions, resulting in delays and frustration.'* Thus governance mechanisms need to be allied to appropriate behaviours if we are to achieve the culture change required.

---

16 Retna, S. (2004) Maximising Return on IT Investments With Enterprise Portfolio Management: Part 1, *Computerworld Management*, Available at: http://www.computerworld.com/ managementtopics/management/project/story/0,10801,98169,00.html [Last accessed: 19th February 2009].

Appropriate Behaviours

Establishing Project Portfolio Management represents a cultural change programme in which managers are asked to: elevate enterprise-level considerations above those of their respective functions and lines of business; adhere to processes that constrain management discretion; ensure the exercise of management judgment is balanced by data and analysis; and to accept greater accountability for results. But if all we do is change the names of the governance body and alter its terms of reference, then we shouldn't be surprised if managers fail to leave their 'silo' hats at the door and behave as usual. Addressing this requires clear communication about the new standards of behaviour expected, leaders that 'walk the talk' and alignment of these standards with the system for reward and recognition. These factors are considered in turn.

1. *Communication and actively engaging those involved in the development of the portfolio management process* – Sanwal (2007)[17] emphasises that '*it is important to educate people on why portfolio management is occurring and what is the benefit*'. At American Express they created a role-playing simulation to help convey the advantages of portfolio management. Ultimately portfolio management both provides and requires transparency and accountability which can cut across managers' autonomy. San Retna from Safeway[18] also recommends high-level workshops as an initial step on the road to a changed managerial mindset, supported by revised processes and systems of reward and recognition.

EXAMPLE 28.   BRITANNIA BUILDING SOCIETY'S 'REALLY BIG PROGRAMME'[1] AND EXPECTED STANDARDS OF BEHAVIOUR

At an early point in the programme, workshops were held to identify the behaviours that would underpin successful delivery. The following behaviours were identified: empathy, a positive attitude and teamwork. The teams met quarterly to review

---

1   Sourced from: National Audit Office (17th November 2006) *Delivering Successful IT-enabled Business Change*, Available at: http://www.nao.org.uk/publications/0607/delivering_successful_it-enabl.aspx [Last accessed: 13th December 2008].

---

17   Sanwal, A. (2007) *Optimizing Corporate Portfolio Management*, John Wiley, Hoboken, New Jersey.
18   San Retna is a vastly experienced Project Portfolio Management practitioner and driving force behind the activities of the Enterprise Portfolio Management Council (EPMC) in the United States. These comments were sourced from conversations with the author in June 2008.

whether they were displaying the key behaviours and to agree any changes that needed to be made. Placing an emphasis on behaviour as well as process and structure was highlighted as a key success factor in the programme's nomination for the British Computer Society's Business Achievement Award.

2.   *Leaders that 'walk the talk'* – consistently exhibiting the expected behaviours and empowering others to call out non-compliance wherever and whenever it occurs, irrespective of seniority. Sanwal (2007)[19] identifies several characters that we need to beware of:

   - the *'closer'* who argues for his/her projects on the basis of charisma, past success and personal relationships;

   - the 'screamer' who's advocacy is based on the 'decibels' rather than the data;

   - the *'end-arounder'* who goes to straight to the top, bypassing the portfolio management process;

   - the *'strategist'* whose sole justification for an investment is some unarticulated and unquantified strategic contribution;

   - the *'doomsdayer'* who's advocacy of a project is premised on fear of what would happen if the investment is not made; and

   - the *'optimist'* who ignores sunk costs and past history believing it will all turn out right in the end.

   The reality is that implementing change is rarely easy or without complications. The leader's actions and behaviour are therefore crucial in demonstrating commitment to the new ways of working and that there's 'no going back'.

3.   *Aligning the reward and recognition systems with the new behaviours* – if we say that a corporate perspective is now expected, but the focus of the performance appraisal system remains on functional or

---

19 Sanwal, A. (2007) *Optimizing Corporate Portfolio Management*, John Wiley, Hoboken, New Jersey.

line of business responsibilities, then we send a clear message that despite what we say, it remains, 'business as usual'. Recruitment, development, reward, recognition and promotion systems therefore need to formally recognise the behaviours identified as underpinning the organisation's portfolio management process such as: pursuing organisational-level aims over functional or line of business objectives; transparent and open reporting; and accountability for performance in an environment built on planning for success rather than attributing blame.

Chapter 7 Conclusions and Take-aways

1. Implementation of Project Portfolio Management is best achieved incrementally starting with basic key processes and building on what already exists within the organisation, before moving on to more advanced processes. This is not an overnight change – embedding portfolio management can take several years.

2. Factors identified as important in sustaining progress include: involving business executives from the start; continuity in key personnel; and training of key personnel on an ongoing basis. A Project Portfolio Management Office (with trained staff) able to provide independent advice, support and analysis to governance boards and projects can also play a crucial role in implementing portfolio management and sustaining progress. Similarly, automation of processes can help embed them as business as usual.

3. Achieving the full benefits of Project Portfolio Management, however, also requires that we look beyond processes to:

    •   *effective governance* – the governance framework needs to be clearly understood by those involved; should be active and based on searching out value rather than passively saying 'yes' or 'no' to potential investments; should involve both robust scrutiny and challenge, as well as support; with clear accountability (including for benefits realisation) reflected in individuals' personal objectives; and needs to be disciplined

– to ensure processes are applied consistently, with checks in place to address non-compliance;

- *appropriate behaviours* – supporting a pan-portfolio perspective which in turn depends on leadership, ongoing communication, training, and realignment of the recruitment, reward and recognition systems; and

- an acceptance that progress requires commitment, patience, tenacity and grit!

8

Measuring Success

'What gets measured gets done'

Anonymous

After reading this chapter you will:

- recognise that portfolio maturity will vary from organisation to organisation and consequently a flexible diagnostic approach has advantages over fixed process maturity assessments;
- understand how assessments of portfolio management maturity can encompass the dimensions of governance and behaviour as well as process as addressed in Chapter 7;
- be aware of the types of performance metrics that can be used to assess not only portfolio management maturity but also impact.

Introduction

So far we have seen that portfolio management has a crucial role to play in managing the transformational change programme, by providing a framework for improving delivery and by ensuring the portfolio continues to represent the best use of resources in pursuit of strategic priorities in a dynamic environment. Nevertheless, the full potential benefits can take time to realise as they are dependent on a shift in both 'locus' and 'focus' of attention – from silo-based investment management, where attention is on the initial investment decision and benefits are considered after implementation, to an organisation-wide, strategy-driven perspective, where investment decisions are incremental in nature, are revisited on a regular basis and where concern with value creation runs throughout the process. For most, this represents a culture change in itself and, as we have seen, sustainability is often a real issue. It is here that performance measurement can play an important role in reflecting the management adage, *'what gets measured gets done'* – this may not always be entirely or exclusively true, but measurement nevertheless plays an important role in communicating the priorities of the change programme and by providing a means to assess and reinforce progress. It can also help win support by demonstrating impact and payback in terms of organisational process efficiency and project outcomes, so addressing the *'what's in it for me'* question.

But what to measure? Most Project Portfolio Management texts and guides include reference to a maturity framework against which organisations are encouraged to assess themselves and use in planning their road map for development. There are however a number of issues in using these maturity models and we explore these further below. More significantly I also argue that consideration needs to be given to how we measure the performance of the change portfolio as a whole – process is important but only if it leads to results. I therefore conclude with some consideration of how the performance of the portfolio can be assessed, whilst remembering that not everything that can be counted counts, and not everything that counts can be counted.

Portfolio Process Metrics – Maturity Frameworks

Maturity frameworks originate from the Capability Maturity Models developed by the Software Engineering Institute at Carnegie Mellon University. These models provide a repeatable, criteria-based evaluation process that: facilitates comparisons over time and provide an incentive to, and road map for, improvement. Applying this approach to the area of project portfolio management has proved popular with maturity frameworks being developed:

- By government agencies such as the United States General Accounting Office's ITIM Framework, the OGC's P3M3 model, and the Project Portfolio Management framework developed at Cambridgeshire County Council for Local Authority use by the Office of the Deputy Prime Minister.

- From academic research – for example, the framework proposed by Jeffery and Leliveld from their research at MIT Sloan[1] and that

---

1   Jeffery, M. and Leliveld, I. (2004) 'Best Practices in IT Portfolio Management', *MIT Sloan Management Review*, Spring 2004, 45:3, pp. 41–49.

derived from the research by Reyck et al. at London and Ashridge Business Schools.[2]

- By industry research and professional organisations such as Gartner (the 'Project Portfolio Maturity Model'), the ISACA's VAL IT framework, the PMIs OPM3 model and IBM's Business Consulting Services' Self Assessment of IT investment management capabilities.

Most of the models are relatively similar with three, four or five maturity levels being organised around between six and a dozen elements of portfolio management (prioritisation, segmentation, reporting and so on). Progress in most is incremental from one stage to the next with a requirement that an organisation achieve all aspects of a level before moving on to the next.

It was noted in Chapter 1 that the imperative to evaluate interventions often does not extend to the frameworks used to manage those interventions. Consequently, it should not come as a great surprise that little formal evaluation of project portfolio management maturity frameworks has taken place to date. There is, however, at least an empirical basis for some of the frameworks proposed – Jeffery and Leliveld's and Reyck et al.'s frameworks for example, were derived from their academic research, and the US Government's ITIM model has been refreshed in the light of practical experience and extensive peer review. That said, I am unaware[3] of any maturity framework having been exposed to robust and serious evaluation – Jeffery and Leliveld themselves (2004) report that, *'Several consulting companies and US federal government agencies have proposed ITPM maturity models. However, none has rigorously validated the frameworks with research data.'* This is something of a shortcoming since these models usually claim to reflect best practice – but in reality a form of best practice that has not been evaluated to demonstrate a positive impact apparently! Consequently it could be argued that their proponents have much in common with snake oil salesmen in the Wild West – a point worth bearing in mind the next time someone encourages you to undertake a portfolio maturity assessment.

---

2   Reyck, B. D., Grushka-Cockayne, Y., Lockett, M., Calderini, S. R., Moura, M. and Sloper, A. (2005) 'The Impact of Project Portfolio Management on Information Technology Projects', *International Journal of Project Management*, 23: February 2005, pp. 524–537.

3   Based on enquiries made with the owners of most of the maturity frameworks referred to in February and March 2008.

Besides the absence of robust evaluation, there are other problems with many of the existing portfolio maturity models. We have already discussed in Chapter 2 the problems with those models that see portfolio management in a fixed hierarchy linked to project and programme management which logically means you shouldn't consider whether you are doing the right projects until you have addressed all relevant delivery issues. Other issues concern:

- most focus on process, but the last chapter highlighted the need to move beyond process to consider issues of behaviour and governance;

- some frameworks, especially those covering project, programme and portfolio perspectives can be, as Makleff and Angelino say, *'voluminous and typically difficult to put into practice in the field.'*[4] Which in turn means that organisations struggle to utilise them effectively – assessments may be undertaken but reports quickly gather dust with little action being taken; and

- research and practical experience indicates that the ideal level of maturity is organisation specific and that preset definitions of maturity are of limited value. Killen et al.[5] for example conclude that, *'The appropriateness of such rigid hierarchies is challenged due to the established need for portfolio management processes to be customized and tailored to the individual environment and the fact that interactions between elements are not adequately considered by such models.'* This need for flexibility in implementation is also *'reinforced by findings throughout the empirical literature'*. Saying that an organisation is at level 3 or 4 for example, is of limited value and can be misleading – in practice, the degree of maturity will vary across the various dimensions or elements.

I therefore propose an approach based on a diagnostic model that encompasses the four portfolio management processes discussed in Chapters 3–6, augmented by consideration of the governance and behavioural dimensions covered in Chapter 7. This provides a clear line of sight across the portfolio management regime. Furthermore it is based on key principles

---

4   Makleff, G. and Angelino, M. (2008) A Proven Paradigm for Creating Enterprise Project and Portfolio Management Adoption Roadmaps that work! UMT (2008).

5   Killen, C. P., Hunt, R. A. and Kleinschmidt, E. J. (2007) *Managing the New Product Development Project Portfolio: A Review of the Literature and Empirical Evidence Proceedings of Portland International Conference on Managing Engineering and Technology (PICMET) 2007*, Portland, Oregon.

rather than preset fixed definitions of what constitutes, for example, level 3 as opposed to level 4 in 'Investment Management'. In this way, the model is used not to assess an organisation against a definition of what maturity means at each level, but rather to engage key stakeholders in a dialogue to determine what good looks like for an organisation given its specific circumstances at a point in time. This framework has been developed from a review of the 'best of the best' frameworks, including those derived from academic research, and has been further developed and enhanced from experience in implementing portfolio management approaches in the UK Government (see Figure 8.1).

Under each key process, governance and behavioral dimension, a series of key principles are stated against which the organisation is invited to assess itself on a scale from 'strongly agree' to 'strongly disagree'. The results are aggregated for each key process and dimension, and can be presented in a 'spider' diagram, or radar chart, to graphically illustrate the relative position across the six dimensions. The organisation can then set target levels for improvement, supported by action plans and indicators of success. These should include both quantitative and qualitative data as well as 'evidence' or 'confirmation' events' (that is, descriptions of how the world will be different that are verifiable) – collectively such measures and indicators should provide tangible evidence, in due course, that the desired improvements have been achieved and so support periodic reassessment using the diagnostic assessment model.

Figure 8.1   The change portfolio diagnostic assessment model

What should be clear is that the portfolio management process will develop over time to reflect the organisation's strategic challenges, its competence in managing the change portfolio and the environment in which it operates. The adoption of a 'champion-challenger' model is therefore recommended whereby participants are actively encouraged to propose enhancements to the process ('challengers') which if accepted, become the new 'champion' process to be used by all. The Change Portfolio Diagnostic Assessment Model is included as Appendix 1 to this chapter.

Portfolio Performance Measurement

Whilst diagnostics and maturity frameworks are useful in assessing process, it is crucial that we are able to measure the performance of the portfolio as a whole – so that we can assess progress in implementing the transformational change programme and take corrective action where required. Appropriately designed measurement systems are not passive – they can also contribute to delivery by providing the data to inform actions and help change behaviours by redirecting effort and by communicating what management considers important. To achieve this metrics should:

1. Relate to the strategic objectives of the portfolio and be tailored to:

   • the various types of investment (or portfolio segment) – cost savings, revenue generation, time savings or performance impact; and

   • stage in the project life cycle, for example, attractiveness and achievability during the planning phase, earned value during delivery, and usage and benefits realised post-implementation.

2. Should be limited in number – but with the facility to 'drill down' to understand the features and causes of variations in more detail. The exception principle should be used in performance reporting – with variances beyond preset tolerance levels being highlighted for management attention.

3. Encompass both quantitative and qualitative (including user feedback) measures and indicators.

One point to emphasise is that yes, this includes metrics relating to individual projects and programmes, but in addition we also need to look at the performance of the portfolio as a whole. In addition to measuring management satisfaction with the process and its outcomes, I recommend that the suite of metrics should encompass both leading and lagging indicators covering four key dimensions of project portfolio performance:

- *DELIVERY* – overall project and programme success rates and empirical levels of optimism bias in relation to capital cost, project duration and operating cost (benefits realisation is covered below under Impact).

- *EFFICIENCY* – from:

  - improved process efficiency – portfolio management can realise efficiency savings in business case preparation, investment appraisal, project evaluation and so on; and

  - more effective resource utilisation, that is, usage of the organisation's pool of skilled project and programme managers. Establishment of an enhanced in-house capability has enabled Manchester City Council, for example, to reduce its reliance on consultants and contractors.

- *BALANCE* – in terms of: overall achievability/deliverability; risk; project life cycle stage; investment type and objective; and flexibility – the extent to which projects and programmes are modular or incremental so that funding can be reallocated if required without significant loss of value.

- *IMPACT* – contribution to strategic objectives and are we achieving the impact and benefits anticipated? At the most basic level, the organisation should track benefits realised against plan and changes in the benefits forecast. These benefits should be analysed:

  - by type – financial savings; time savings; revenue generated; costs avoided; and strategic impact and so on; and

  - by source – from improved procurement; economies of scale; productivity; eliminating duplication; business change/process re-engineering and so on.

There are also a number of lead indicators mentioned in the previous chapters that organisations should also monitor – including movement of projects and programmes towards the upper-right quadrant of the 'Attractiveness-Achievability' portfolio map shown in Chapter 5 and:

- the percentage of business cases that recommend not investing;

- the number of project proposals that are rejected at each stage or phase gate review; and

- funding reallocated at each portfolio-level review.

In each case there is no guide to what good performance looks like other than that the answer in most cases should be more than zero – if not, it is a warning signal that the funnel is becoming a tunnel and that the process is becoming a bureaucracy without effective action being taken in the light of changed circumstances and lessons learned.

A key point to note is that these metrics should be used not only *ex post* in managing the portfolio of change initiatives, but also *ex ante* – in appraising and prioritising investments for inclusion in the portfolio. In this way, an organisationally appropriate, standard suite of metrics can be developed and used from project selection, through delivery, to benefits realisation – although as noted above, the actual metrics used will vary depending on the stage of the project life cycle of each initiative.

Chapter 8 Conclusions and Take-aways

1. Many Portfolio Management maturity frameworks have been developed and most are incremental (progress is stage by stage) and have four or five levels organised around between six and a dozen key elements of portfolio management. But:

   - little formal evaluation of these frameworks has been undertaken to demonstrate correlation between process maturity and performance;

   - most focus on process without also considering the crucial dimensions of behaviour and governance; and

- research indicates that the ideal level of maturity is organisation specific, that preset definitions of maturity are of limited value and the degree of 'maturity' will vary across the various dimensions as well as the defined levels.

2. A diagnostic assessment model is therefore recommended that encompasses process, governance and behavioural dimensions and that, rather than evaluating the organisation against a preset definition of what maturity means at each level, engages the organisation in a dialogue to determine what good looks like for the organisation given its specific circumstances at a point in time. This model has been developed from a review of the 'best of the best' frameworks, and relevant research and practical experience in developing project portfolio management in the UK Government (see Appendix 1 to this chapter).

3. In addition to measuring process maturity, it is also crucial that the effectiveness of portfolio management and the performance of the change portfolio as a whole is assessed to provide a clear line of sight from strategic intent through to benefits realisation. This includes measures and indicators of management satisfaction as well as: delivery, efficiency, balance and impact.

Appendix to Chapter 8 – Change Portfolio Diagnostic Assessment Model

PORTFOLIO NAME

Portfolio Management Processes and Dimensions	Strongly Agree	Agree	Disagree	Strongly Disagree
Overarching Dimension – Governance and Controls				
1. Senior management are active in the management of the portfolio.				
2. An Investment Management Committee has been established to exercise oversight of the portfolio as a whole.				
3. Key stakeholders are able to explain the governance framework i.e. what decisions are made, where, by whom and what factors/criteria are employed.				
4. The governance process incorporates both challenge and support in an active process of planning for success rather than blame attribution.				
5. There is cross-organisational cooperation and participation – all affected areas are involved in managing the portfolio.				
6. Actions are taken promptly to address performance issues, manage portfolio risk and to maintain an optimum allocation of funds. Entries on the Issues Log are addressed promptly.				
7. The efficiency and effectiveness of the portfolio governance process is reviewed at least annually (involvement by an independent non-executive is advised).				
8. An appropriate balance exists between exercise of managerial judgment and the use of analytical, data driven, evidence-based decision making.				
Supporting Dimension – Culture and Behaviours				
1. Expected standards of behaviour (e.g. pursuing organizational-level aims over functional or line of business objectives; transparent and open reporting; and accountability for performance in an environment built on planning for success rather than attributing blame) are clearly articulated and adhered to.				

Portfolio Management Processes and Dimensions	Strongly Agree	Agree	Disagree	Strongly Disagree
2. Senior management consistently demonstrate a commitment to managing the portfolio in the interests of the organisation as a whole.				
3. The performance management system (including rewards and recognition) is aligned with the expected standards of behaviour.				
4. There is a clear and sustained commitment to open, accurate and transparent reporting on project/programme performance based on the principle of 'one version of the truth'.				
5. There is a clear and sustained commitment to communicating the rationale behind portfolio decisions.				
Key Process 1. Establishing the Portfolio				
1.1 Establishing the scope of the portfolio				
1. The objectives of the Portfolio (and strategic targets and priorities to which the portfolio is expected to contribute) are clearly defined.				
2. There are common and accepted definitions of what constitutes a project and a programme (as opposed to 'business as usual').				
3. The scope/boundaries of the portfolio are clearly defined in terms of: • what types of activity/project are included and excluded; and • size/cost thresholds for inclusion in the portfolio.				
4. Portfolio definitions and thresholds are enforced consistently and effectively.				
5. There is a clear view of the projects/activities that are within the scope of the portfolio, their costs and benefits.				
1.2 Implementing standardised processes, templates and guidance				
1. Guidance exists covering project submissions, from feasibility study through business cases to project closure, encompassing format, expected content and required approval level.				
2. Staff responsible for preparing project submissions are aware of the guidance and templates, and training provision in the use of the organisation's Portfolio Management process is available.				

Portfolio Management Processes and Dimensions	Strongly Agree	Agree	Disagree	Strongly Disagree
3. Business case templates include the requirement for: a clear and succinct statement of the investment justification; the benefits (financial benefits and/or strategic impact); reliable estimates of cost (upfront and running costs); and realistic estimates of achievability (encompassing technical and project delivery and likelihood of benefits realisation).				
4. Processes adopt a 'Champion-Challenger' approach whereby participants are actively encouraged to propose enhancements to the process which if accepted, become the new 'champion' process to be used by all.				
1.3 Investment criteria				
1. Investment criteria for deciding where to invest (and reinvest) are clearly defined.				
2. Investment criteria used are appropriate to the category of project e.g. projects with a cost saving/revenue enhancing driver are appraised on a NPV basis; projects with a strategic driver are appraised on the basis of strategic contribution per £ invested; mandatory projects on the basis of lowest net present cost etc.				
3. Standard processes exist for assessing investment 'Attractiveness' (e.g. NPV, Strategic Contribution Analysis etc).				
4. Standard processes exist for assessing investment 'Achievability'.				
1.4 Portfolio Segmentation				
1. The portfolio is divided into appropriate segments to aid resource allocation.				
2. Appropriate investment criteria are set for each segment.				
Key Process 2. Investment Management				
2.1 Investment appraisal				
1. The organisation's business cases represent a reliable assessment of the case for each project and fairly appraise the options.				
2. Business cases are developed independently of the project team and those responsible for project delivery.				

Portfolio Management Processes and Dimensions	Strongly Agree	Agree	Disagree	Strongly Disagree
3. System requirements/functionality are agreed with/validated by front line users.				
4. Investment decisions consider return/ attractiveness in the context of risk/achievability and affordability.				
5. Assessments of 'Attractiveness' are robust and based on appropriate evidence: • financial and efficiency benefits are valued in accordance with organisational rules and are agreed e.g. by the Finance function and/or efficiency planners; • strategic, performance or effectiveness benefits are supported by an appropriately detailed Strategic Contribution Analysis (linking project benefits to strategic success measures) and are agreed e.g. with the organisation's strategic planning function.				
6. Assessments of 'Achievability' are realistic and encompass both project/technical deliverability and realisation of benefits.				
7. Investment Appraisals take into consideration portfolio-level criteria such as the reuse/ exploitation of components and organisational capability/capacity.				
8. Investment Appraisals take into consideration whether the project has adopted a phased or modular approach in which benefits are tied to each phase/module so providing greater flexibility in future portfolio-level funding allocations.				
9. Business case costings are adjusted for optimism bias and sensitivity analysis is undertaken to assess the impact of changes in key variables.				
10. Benefits in business cases are adjusted to reflect the degree of confidence that they will be realised.				
11. Investment decisions are appropriately weighted in terms of data driven analysis and management judgment – investment decisions are informed by past performance i.e. performance in terms of project delivery and benefits realisation is monitored and fed into current appraisals.				

Portfolio Management Processes and Dimensions	Strongly Agree	Agree	Disagree	Strongly Disagree
2.2 Portfolio prioritisation				
1. The rules guiding portfolio prioritisation decisions are documented and understood by all those involved.				
2. Portfolio-level investment decisions take into consideration not only individual investments' 'Attractiveness' and 'Achievability' but also – Affordability i.e. the portfolio is affordable in the short term; the impact on future running costs is considered; and the opportunity cost of allocating funds now versus retaining some as a contingency for new ideas and cost escalation is taken into account.				
3. Portfolio-level investment decisions take into consideration not only individual investments' 'Attractiveness' and 'Achievability' but also Flexibility i.e. the extent to which projects are modular or phased so that funding can be adjusted to reflect changed circumstances without wasting previous investments.				
4. Portfolio-level investment decisions take into consideration not only individual investments' 'Attractiveness' and 'Achievability' but also overall portfolio balance in terms of: <ul><li>project life cycle i.e. a pipeline of projects at various stages in their life cycles;</li><li>the cumulative business change impact of the portfolio is reasonable;</li><li>long-term investments that support the creation of capability and capacity and projects with a more immediate impact;</li><li>risk – the overall risk of the portfolio is acceptable in terms of attractiveness/ achievability;</li><li>the organisation is not overly exposed to one or more suppliers; and</li><li>coverage of all strategic priorities.</li></ul>				
5. Portfolio-level investment decisions take into consideration not only individual investments' 'Attractiveness' and 'Achievability' but also Capability – the organisation has the skills and resources to deliver the portfolio as a whole.				

Portfolio Management Processes and Dimensions	Strongly Agree	Agree	Disagree	Strongly Disagree
6. Portfolio-level investment decisions take into consideration not only individual investments' 'Attractiveness' and 'Achievability' but also Dependencies e.g. where infrastructure investments may score poorly in attractiveness terms but they enable a number of attractive applications.				
Key Process 3. Managing the Portfolio 'in flight'				
3.1 Managing innovation – managing the portfolio entry point				
1. A forward view of potential projects/initiatives is maintained.				
2. The start of projects/initiatives is managed in a structured manner (e.g. via a 'Start Gate') with a formal screening and approval process for idea investigation so that the portfolio does not become gridlocked with too many initiatives or alternatively a pipeline that dries up.				
3.2 Managing the project funnel via a phase/stage gate process				
1. An effective phase/stage gate process operates with funding allocated in incremental budgetary envelopes to take the project through to the next review.				
2. Looking back – gate reviews consider performance since the last review in terms of: spend versus budget and progress versus plan.				
3. Looking forward – gate reviews consider the revised cost/benefit position and what actions are required to ensure successful project delivery and benefits realisation.				
4. Continued funding is dependent on performance, continued strategic contribution and formal recommitment to benefits realisation. Where performance falls below plan and/or conditions change, there is a presumption that funding will be reallocated unless a compelling case is made to continue.				
5. The outcome of gate reviews is a clear (and documented) decision to: 'Continue to next gate' 'Stop/Hold' or 'Kill', with any conditions being recorded.				

Portfolio Management Processes and Dimensions	Strongly Agree	Agree	Disagree	Strongly Disagree
3.3 Periodic portfolio-level reviews – to ensure the portfolio remains strategically aligned and balanced				
1. Portfolio-level reviews are held on a regular basis (at least annually) to assess continued strategic alignment, balance, performance, resource utilisation and that the portfolio continues to represent the most cost-effective allocation of funds.				
2. The portfolio is a 'funnel' rather than a 'tunnel' with funding being reallocated as organisational learning improves and in the light of changed circumstances.				
3. The project pipeline is reviewed to ensure that it has sufficient quality and numbers of projects and conversely, that the portfolio is not facing gridlock.				
4. Business case adequacy is reviewed on a periodic basis and deficiencies in preparation are corrected (e.g. by training, adoption of more robust tools and techniques).				
5. Failing and non-strategically aligned projects are stopped promptly to avoid further wasted expenditure.				
6. Even when performance is satisfactory, where required, funds are reallocated and projects rescheduled in the interests of the portfolio as a whole.				
7. Lessons learned from post-implementation reviews are monitored and addressed.				
3.4 Regular progress reporting – to provide a 'clear line of sight' from strategic intent through to benefits realisation				
1. A standard suite of metrics has been developed encompassing project and programme performance and the performance of the portfolio as a whole.				
2. Governance bodies receive regular (usually at least monthly) progress reports encompassing progress (cost versus budget and progress versus planned milestones) on the major projects, programmes and initiatives in the portfolio.				

Portfolio Management Processes and Dimensions	Strongly Agree	Agree	Disagree	Strongly Disagree
3. Governance bodies receive regular progress reports on portfolio-level metrics. For example: benefits realised against plan; resource utilisation; spend versus budget; key portfolio-level delivery and benefits realisation risks; portfolio balance; pipeline analysis – funnel project shape and size (number of projects at each stage), attrition rate, throughput speed; etc.				
4. Portfolio data is complete, credible and accepted (one version of the truth).				
3.5 Constraint, resource and dependency management				
1. Dependencies and interdependencies between projects and programmes are actively managed at a portfolio level.				
2. Project Managers and other skilled resources are managed as a 'pool' for the benefits of the portfolio as a whole; capacity is managed to match demand; and proficiency levels match project criticality.				
Key Process 4. Value Management				
1. A consistent approach to benefits identification is used across the portfolio – guidance on the classification, quantification, valuation and validation of benefits is used consistently to enable comparative analysis and reporting.				
2. Wherever possible forecast benefits are booked in organisational efficiency plans, strategic targets etc.				
3. Projects, programmes and initiatives have a comprehensive Benefits Realisation Plan.				
4. Benefits realisation is managed at a portfolio or enterprise level with regular reporting on benefits against plan at a portfolio level.				
5. Benefits realisation is integrated into the organisation's Performance Management framework with accountability for benefits realisation clearly defined.				
6. Benefits Management is accepted as a joint responsibility between project and operational/business management (but with the latter taking the lead).				

Portfolio Management Processes and Dimensions	Strongly Agree	Agree	Disagree	Strongly Disagree
7. Where benefits fall behind trajectory effective action is taken to address the shortfall.				
8. All projects and programmes have post-implementation reviews which are undertaken with a focus on organisational learning (and processes are amended in the light of such learnings).				
9. The focus of the benefits management regime is on value creation with continual learning and further exploitation of capability beyond project closure.				

9

Conclusions

'The secret of success is constancy to purpose.'

Benjamin Disraeli

We set out to assess the case for using Project Portfolio Management in managing our investments in change. We found there is a strong case, supported by academic and industry research, for using Project Portfolio Management to:

- improve the appraisal and prioritisation of initiatives against organisational priorities;

- manage these investments 'in flight' to maintain strategic alignment in the context of internal constraints, project dependencies and environmental change; and

- optimise the return on investment by realising benefits in practice.

We saw that Project Portfolio Management can reduce costs, enable project and programme delivery, and reduce risk – just establishing an enterprise-wide view of all project activity can deliver substantial financial benefits from removal of redundant, duplicate and poorly performing projects and from gaining an insight into how investments in one part of the organisation can be reused elsewhere. Additional benefits are linked with increasing portfolio process maturity and active management of the portfolio, but such benefits are often more difficult to measure in financial terms since they concern improved strategic contribution and a more balanced and achievable portfolio.

Realisation of these potential benefits is, however, far from automatic, and those that start by purchasing a software solution usually find progress to be slow. Establishing organisationally appropriate portfolio management processes and governance regimes come first, and progress is built on the foundations of four crucial prerequisites:

1. A clearly articulated corporate strategy – so that we can move beyond strategic alignment, to reliably and consistently appraise the *contribution* of initiatives to organisational strategy.

2. Top management support – to demonstrate clearly that there's no going back and that management expect the change portfolio to be managed in the interests of the organisation as a whole.

3. A skilled portfolio analysis function – to develop and manage the portfolio processes and undertake independent, competent and credible investment appraisals and portfolio prioritisation exercises.

4. Modular or incremental project development and deployment – so that funding can be reallocated to reflect project performance and shifts in organisational priorities in the light of environmental changes.

These factors lay the basis for effective implementation of project portfolio management which is best approached incrementally, starting with basic key processes and building on what already exists within the organisation. This is no overnight change – embedding Portfolio Management as 'business as usual' can take several years, but rapid progress can be made by learning from the experience of others. Factors identified as important in sustaining progress include:

1. involving business executives from the start – so that it is seen to be business-led and not perceived as a Project and Programme Management or IT initiative;

2. continuity in key personnel – to maintain focus and ensure that the initiative is not seen as something associated with the previous regime;

3. training of key personnel on an ongoing basis – so that progress is not impacted by staff turnover;

4. as above, a Project Portfolio Management function (actual or virtual) able to provide independent advice, support and analysis to the governance bodies and business units;

5. the use of appropriate software tools to streamline the process and help sustain progress by embedding repeatable portfolio management processes as 'business as usual'; and

6. embedding Project Portfolio Management in the organisation's planning, resource management and performance management regimes – the process of measuring performance from a portfolio perspective can help embed portfolio management as part of the corporate routine. Measurement of portfolio performance encompasses two dimensions:

- process maturity – a diagnostic assessment approach is recommended, going beyond process to consider the dimensions of governance and behaviour;

> **Tip 1 – establish a champion-challenger model where business units are actively encouraged to propose enhancements to the process ('challengers') which if accepted, become the new 'champion' process to be used by all. But until that point, everyone uses the currently approved 'champion' process.**

- portfolio performance in terms of: delivery, efficiency, balance and impact.

There are four key Project Portfolio Management processes – establishing the change portfolio; investment management and portfolio prioritisation; managing the portfolio 'in flight'; and benefits management.

Key Process 1: Establishing the Change Portfolio

This addresses four key areas.

1. Deciding on the scope of the portfolio – which projects, programmes and other change initiatives will be included and which are excluded from the portfolio. On the one hand beware overload from hundreds of initiatives, and on the other, watch out for deliberate disaggregation of proposals to avoid portfolio governance.

> **Tip 2** – base the criteria for inclusion in the change portfolio *on impact not cost*, that is all initiatives with a material contribution to organisational strategy should be included in the change portfolio. Remember we invest in change to realise benefits – so manage benefits as robustly as you do costs.

2.   Agreeing standardised processes, templates and guidance – take the opportunity to streamline documentation to focus on the key data and shift the focus from costs to value. Business cases should *'start with the end in mind'*.

> **Tip 3** – ensure *all* the costs required to realise the benefits claimed are included in the business case, even when they fall on different budgets.

> **Tip 4** – introduce a summary business case template capturing the salient information on project attractiveness and achievability in a common format. Remember, size is the enemy of understanding, so introduce short summary documentation with detailed analyses available if required.

3.   Determining the investment criteria that will be used to select and prioritise investments.

> **Tip 5** – don't agonise in selecting your investment criteria. A basic set can be developed easily and quickly.

4.   Segmenting the portfolio – splitting the portfolio into organisationally appropriate categories, for example, by project type and/or investment objective – and then tailoring the investment criteria to the various portfolio segments.

> **Tip 6** – divide the portfolio into segments relating to the four generic investment objectives: to save money or improve efficiency; to generate income; to contribute to an organisational strategy; or because we have to in response to a legal, regulatory or political requirement, or to maintain business as usual.

Key Process 2. Investment Management

There are six key points to note here.

1. Treating projects, programmes and other change initiatives as INVESTMENTS – yes focus on cost control and project delivery, but above all focus on benefits and make the implicit assumptions that appear in business cases, explicit.

Tip 7 – cut to the chase and be clear about what benefits you are buying from any investment in change, that is, how much money or time will be saved (and if time – what will it be used for), revenue generated, or exactly what contribution to strategic targets or business priorities will we get and how exactly will we know that the benefits have been realised?

---

2. In appraising potential projects for investment, consider project attractiveness (return) in the context of their achievability (risk).

Tip 8 – investment criteria should be tailored to the investment objective:

- **for projects that are designed to reduce costs or increase revenue use financial measures (NPV, IRR, payback and so on);**
- **for strategic projects use Strategic Contribution Analysis to understand the logic behind performance-enhancing benefits, the scale of the anticipated impact and confidence that they will be realised; and**
- **for mandatory projects – use lowest cost to meet the requirements.**

Tip 9 – measures of achievability should encompass project and technical deliverability as well as likelihood of benefits realisation (see templates included as an Appendix to Chapter 4).

---

3. Financial approaches are the most common approach to investment appraisal but they have several weaknesses. Firstly, they are premised on accurate estimates of costs and benefits, yet research shows estimates are often a lot less accurate than we'd like to believe – 'optimism bias' and 'strategic misrepresentation' are a reality. Secondly, they risk obscuring the real nature of the investment and its benefits, particularly where the benefits are non-financial in

nature. Thirdly, empirical research indicates that they can lead to poor decision making. So triangulate investment appraisals – use multiple 'value lens' and combine financial appraisals with MCA, Strategic Contribution Analysis, management scorecards and decision conferencing to build consensus around the process and the investments chosen.

Tip 10 – use multiple 'value lens' to triangulate investment appraisals: economic cost-benefit appraisal enhanced by financial appraisal, Strategic Contribution Analysis, as well as MCA scorecards.

---

4.   Validating forecasts by spending more time upfront doing your homework, augmenting 'inside view' forecasts with an 'outside view', subject investments to independent review and scrutiny, and book benefits wherever possible in budgets, headcount targets, business plans and personal performance agreements; track results and hold business units to account for realising the benefits they have committed to.

Tip 11 – appoint a devil's advocate or 'fool' to challenge the assumptions underpinning business cases and ask:

- **business case writers and sponsors – what's your track record in presenting reliable and accurate forecasts?**
- **the organisation – how many business cases recommend don't invest?**

---

5.   Investments also need to be appraised from a portfolio-level perspective, that is, taking into account dependencies between projects, organisational constraints including capacity to absorb change, and affordability. Ask – is the overall portfolio balanced in terms of: strategic coverage; in terms of short and longer-term investments; are risks at a portfolio level acceptable; and is it sufficiently flexible to enable funding reallocations in response to project performance, organisational learning and environmental change without significant loss of investment?

6.   Portfolio Management is both an art as well as a science – use data-driven analysis to inform the exercise of management judgment.

> **Tip 12** – track the organisation's performance in delivering projects on time and to budget and in realising benefits – and use this performance data to inform forecasting and the appraisal of potential investments. Don't just kill failing projects, address the underlying causes.

Key Process 3: Managing the Portfolio 'In Flight'

Things rarely go exactly to plan and conditions, and therefore business priorities, change. Consequently the portfolio needs to be managed 'in flight' to maintain strategic alignment, portfolio balance and ensure the overall level of risk remains acceptable. This process should be active, value-driven and premised on 'planning for success' with joint accountability for performance, rather than 'after the event' accountability.

Four key elements in this process were identified:

1. Managing the portfolio entry point – using a structured, disciplined start gate process to ensure that on the one hand the portfolio has a stream of new ideas to investigate, and on the other, it doesn't become overwhelmed by new projects.

2. Project stage/phase gates reviews – linking funding to performance and ensuring that these gates 'have teeth' so that the funnel does not become a tunnel.

> **Tip 13** – establish a clear presumption that if projects go outside of tolerance, funding ceases. Project Managers and Business Sponsors can argue for continued funding but the case needs to be made.

3. Periodic portfolio-level reviews – monitoring the performance of the portfolio of change, ensuring continued strategic alignment, and assessing the effectiveness of the portfolio management processes themselves.

4. Regular portfolio-level progress reporting – with a bias for action so that even 'no action' is a deliberate management decision.

> **Tip 14 – employ 'one version of the truth' reporting based on a standard template of information required and a schedule for data submission.**

Key Portfolio Process 4: Benefits or Value Management

Benefits realisation starts with the business case – research shows that failing programmes rarely have strong business cases. Optimism bias and strategic misrepresentation are a reality – so ensure benefit claims are:

- *robust,* by checking that they are consistent with the organisation's guidelines for quantifying and valuing benefits. Challenge the assumptions that masquerade as facts; and

- *realisable,* by agreeing them with the recipients. Wherever possible 'book' the benefits by adjusting unit budgets, reducing target unit costs, including them in headcount reductions, or by reflecting them in the organisation's and individuals' performance targets. But also check that efficiencies are real and that output and service quality does not suffer from creating unfunded pressures.

> **Tip 15 – move beyond hurdle rates of return by asking not only has a potential project identified sufficient benefits to justify the investment, but more to the point, have all potential benefits been identified?**

> **Tip 16 – ensure benefits are agreed with recipients BEFORE funding is allocated. Experience shows that reaching agreement post-funding is far more difficult.**

Benefits must be placed at the centre of the investment appraisal and portfolio prioritisation processes – funding should be linked to benefits forecasts and project sponsors should be able to answer the question *'what benefits am I buying?'*

> **Tip 17 – Project gate and portfolio-level reviews should rebaseline the benefits case and culminate in a *formal* recommitment to benefits realisation by the recipient business units.**

Look beyond realising forecast benefits to value creation – benefits are usually dependent on business change and may not be realised until after project deployment has been completed and the project team has disbanded. So plan and manage benefits realisation from a portfolio rather than a project perspective and engage with users to capture and disseminate lessons learned.

> **Tip 18 – be realistic in estimating and enthusiastic in implementing. In regard to the latter, continually ask, 'is that the best we can do?' – challenge managers to identify additional sources of value from the accumulated investment in change.**

Achieving the full benefits of Project Portfolio Management however also requires that we look beyond processes to:

- *Effective governance* – the governance framework needs to be clearly understood by those involved; should be active and based on searching out value rather than passively saying 'yes' or 'no' to potential investments; should involve both robust scrutiny and challenge, as well as support; with clear accountability (including for benefits realisation) reflected in individuals' personal objectives; and needs to be disciplined – to ensure processes are applied consistently, with checks in place to address non-compliance.

> **Tip 19 – effective governance means active involvement and making decisions that impact on delivery, so regularly assess the effectiveness of the governance process and involve non-executives or a 'fool', to provide an independent view.**

- *Appropriate behaviours* – supporting a pan-portfolio perspective which in turn depends on leadership, ongoing communication, training, and realignment of the reward and recognition systems.

> **Tip 20 – clearly define the expected standards of behaviour and empower everyone, irrespective of grade or seniority, to call out any deviation from these standards.**

Above all, remember the advice to '*Keep it simple stupid*' and don't try to run before you can walk. Focus on three fundamentals:

- Are we clear about the benefits we are buying/value being created?

- Have we a clear and transparent line of sight from strategic intent to benefits realisation/value creation to enable 'fast and frugal' decision-making?

- Is there a basis for real accountability based on planning for success?

The lessons of those who have implemented Project Portfolio Management by addressing these three fundamentals are that the rewards are great, and significantly, they are within your grasp.

I am keen to maintain and develop the dialogue with practitioners and to capture learnings wherever they occur – if you have questions, comments or observations, please feel free to contact me at: stephen.jenner@cjit.gsi.gov.uk or Stephen.Jenner5@btinternet.com.

Good luck!

About the Author

Steve has extensive experience of Investment Appraisal, Portfolio Management and Benefits Management in the public sector, primarily the UK, although he has also worked in the public sector in Australia and in both spending departments and the centre. He was the driving force behind the development of the CJS IT approach to Portfolio and Benefits Management that has received international recognition – for example, by Gartner, the European Commission's economics of e-Government project and by the UK Government report to the OECD that referred to it as 'UK Best Practice' – and which won the 2007 Civil Service award for financial management.

From mid-2006, he was Director of Criminal Justice IT, following the appointment of his predecessor, John Suffolk, as the first UK Government CIO. He continues to advise UK Government departments on the development of their approaches to Portfolio and Benefits Management as part of the Transformational Government and Service Transformation agendas. Additionally he provides independent assurance on major government programmes.

Steve is a Fellow of the Chartered Institute of Management Accountants (FCMA), has an MBA and also holds a Masters of Studies degree from Fitzwilliam College, Cambridge University.

Steve is a regular speaker at conferences and training courses on the subjects of Investment Appraisal, Portfolio Prioritisation and Benefits Management. He is also the author of *Realising Benefits from Government ICT investments – A Fool's Errand?* (Academic Publishing, 2009) and co-author with colleagues from the EPMC of *Project Portfolio Management – A View from the Management Trenches* (Wiley, 2009).

Index